Martin Luther King

Pocket BIOGRAPHIES

Series Editor C.S. Nicholls

Highly readable brief lives of those who have played a significant part in history, and whose contributions still influence contemporary culture.

Pocket BIOGRAPHIES

Martin Luther King

HARRY HARMER

SUTTON PUBLISHING

First published in 1998 by
Sutton Publishing Limited · Phoenix Mill
Thrupp · Stroud · Gloucestershire · GL5 2BU

Reprinted in 2002

British Library Cataloguing in Publication Data
A catalogue record for this book is available from the British
Library.

ISBN 0-7509-1932-9

Typeset in 13/18 pt Perpetua.
Typesetting and origination by
Sutton Publishing Limited.
Printed in Great Britain by
J.H. Haynes & Co. Ltd, Sparkford.

CONTENTS

CHRONOLOGY

1929   **15 January**. Michael Luther King (later Martin Luther King Jr) born in Atlanta, Georgia

1944   **20 September**. Enters Morehouse College, Atlanta; graduates as BA in Sociology, June 1948

1948   **25 February**. Ordained and becomes assistant pastor to his father at Ebenezer Baptist Church, Atlanta

September. Enters Crozer Theological Seminary, Chester, Pennsylvania; graduates as Bachelor of Divinity, June 1951; begins postgraduate studies at Boston University in September

1953   **18 June**. Marries Coretta Scott in Marion, Alabama

1954   **17 May.** US Supreme Court ruling on *Brown v Board of Education of Topeka* declares racial segregation unconstitutional

31 October. King installed by father as pastor at Dexter Avenue Baptist Church, Montgomery, Alabama

1955   **5 June**. Receives PhD in Systematic Theology from Boston University

17 November. First child, Yolanda Denise, born

December. Montgomery bus boycott begins; King elected president of Montgomery Improvement Association (MIA)

1956   **30 January**. King's home bombed

21 February. King and MIA leaders arrested for violating Alabama ban on trade boycotts

13 November. US Supreme Court rules Montgomery bus segregation unconstitutional; King among the first passengers on desegregated buses, December

1957   **8–9 January**. Southern Christian Leadership Conference (SCLC) formed with King as president

18 February. King features on *Time* magazine cover

6 March. Attends Ghana independence celebrations

17 May. King calls for black voting rights at Prayer Pilgrimage in Washington DC

9 September. Civil Rights Act establishes a Civil Rights Commission and Department of Justice Civil Rights Division

23 October. King's second child, Martin Luther King III, born

1958   **23 June**. King and other civil rights leaders meet President Eisenhower at the White House

4 September. King convicted of failing to obey a police officer, outside Montgomery's

Recorder's Court, refuses to pay fine but is
released after Police Commissioner pays

17 September. King's first book, *Stride Toward
Freedom: The Montgomery Story*, published

20 September. King is stabbed in Harlem by a
mentally ill woman

1959   **February**. The Kings visit India and meet Prime
Minister Nehru; King studies Gandhi's non-
violent tactics

1960   **24 January**. King becomes co-pastor of
Ebenezer Baptist Church, Atlanta

1 February. Students begin lunch counter sit-
ins in North Carolina; Student Nonviolent
Coordinating Committee (SNCC) founded in
April

24 June. King meets Democratic presidential
candidate John F. Kennedy to discuss racial
issues

19 October. King jailed for participation in
Atlanta sit-in

1961   **30 January**. King's third child, Dexter Scott,
born

4 May. Freedom Rides campaign begins

26 May. King becomes chairman of the
Freedom Riders Co-ordinating Committee

11 December. King in Albany, Georgia, to support
desegregation capaign; arrested on 16 December
for illegally parading

1962   **27 July**. Jailed for leading prayer vigil at Albany
city hall

16 October. Asks President Kennedy to issue a
second Emancipation Proclamation to end racial
segregation

17 December. King and other black leaders
meet President Kennedy to request economic aid
for African states and sanctions against South
Africa

1963   **28 March**. Fourth child, Bernice Albertina,
born

12 April. King jailed for leading banned march
in Birmingham, Alabama; writes 'Letter from
Birmingham Jail' on non-violent civil
disobedience

3–5 May. Police brutally attack protesters in
Birmingham

11 May. King's headquarters and brother's
home bombed

June. King's *Strength to Love* published

28 August. King makes 'I Have a Dream' speech
at March on Washington

10 October. Attorney General Robert F.
Kennedy authorizes Federal Bureau of
Investigation (FBI) wiretapping of King's and
SCLC telephones

3 December. Meets President Lyndon Johnson
to discuss the Civil Rights Bill

1964   **3 January**. *Time* magazine names King 'Man of
the Year'

June. King's *Why We Can't Wait* published

2 July. King present at signing of Civil Rights

Act by President Johnson

20 July. SCLC launches 'People to People' campaign in Mississippi to support SNCC and Congress of Racial Equality voter registration drive

July–August. Riots in Harlem, New Jersey, Illinois and Pennsylvania

18 September. King has audience with Pope Pius VI in Rome

10 December. King receives the Nobel Peace Prize in Oslo

1965 **2 February**. Arrested for participation in Selma voter registration drive

21 February. Malcolm X assassinated

21–5 March. King leads Selma to Montgomery march; addresses 25,000 supporters in Montgomery

6 August. King present at the signing of the Voting Rights Act by President Johnson

11–16 August. 34 dead (28 of whom are black) in rioting in Watts, the Los Angeles black ghetto

August. King calls for negotiated end to the Vietnam war and condemns US bombing of the north

1966 **February**. King and his family move into a Chicago apartment to participate in integration campaign

16 May. King's becomes chairman of Clergy and Laymen Concerned about Vietnam

June. 'Black Power' slogan used publicly for the first time by SNCC leaders in Mississippi

July. King opens campaign to desegregate housing in Chicago

12 July. Rioting on Chicago's West Side

5 August. King stoned by whites while leading anti-segregation demonstration in Chicago

1967   **January**. Writes *Where Do We Go From Here?* in Jamaica

4 April. Delivers anti-Vietnam war speech in New York City; warns of renewed rioting if black grievances are not redressed

June–July. Riots in Boston, Newark and Detroit

August. King is heckled by black activists at a Chicago 'New Politics' conference

27 November. King announces formation of a Poor People's Campaign to march on Washington, DC

1968   **28 March**. Leads march in Memphis, Tennessee, in support of striking sanitation workers

3 April. Delivers 'I've Been to the Mountain Top' speech at Mason Temple, Memphis

4 April. Assassinated at Lorraine Motel, Memphis; rioting erupts throughout the United States

1977   **4 July**. Posthumously awarded the Presidential Medal of Freedom

1983   **2 November**. King's birthday designated a public holiday in the United States

Chronology

1991   **30 June**. Scene of King's assassination becomes a National Civil Rights Museum

ONE

'WE WILL GET TO THE PROMISED LAND'

A little after six in the evening on 4 April 1968 Martin Luther King Jr walked on to the balcony from his room at the Lorraine Motel, Memphis. He joked with supporters in the car park below and talked with a musician about a song King wanted to be performed at a rally that evening, 'Take My Hand, Precious Lord'. A single shot rang out. Hit by a 30.06 bullet King sprawled against the wall, his arms outstretched, then crumpled to the floor. Ralph Abernathy, a friend of thirteen years' standing, cradled King's head as aides tried to staunch the blood gushing from a massive tear in his neck. King died an hour later in hospital.

The night before, King had addressed the Mason Temple congregation and spoke of threats against his life by 'some of our sick white brothers'. Not yet 40, he spoke of his hopes for a long life. 'But I'm not concerned about that now,' he said.

> I just want to do God's will. And He's allowed me to go up to the mountain. And I've looked over. And I've seen the promised land. I may not get there with you. But I want you to know tonight, that we, as a people, will get to the promised land. And I'm happy, tonight. I'm not worried about anything. I'm not fearing any man. Mine eyes have seen the glory of the coming of the Lord.[1]

America's black ghettos were initially dazed at King's death. But, as the news was absorbed, rioting, burning and looting erupted in 125 cities, with gun battles in the streets. 'Go home and get your guns!' Black Power leader Stokely Carmichael told a crowd in Washington DC. 'When the white man comes he is coming to kill you. I don't want any black blood in the street!'[2] In the capital itself seventy fires raged as rioting reached within two blocks of the White House. In the days of rage following King's death, 46 people were killed, 2,600 injured and 22,000 arrested. Over

$45 million worth of property was damaged or destroyed by angry rioters. King had built his life on a gospel of pacifism, preaching to his followers that violence – the weapon of the oppressor – could only undermine the fundamental and undeniable justice of their cause. What had brought America to this?

King's mission was to undo the wrongs of over three hundred years of history. The freeing of the slaves by Lincoln's Emancipation Proclamation in 1863 represented only the first step. King described vividly the black experience in the New World. 'Abused and scorned though we may be, our destiny is tied up with the destiny of America,' he wrote from prison in 1963.

> Before the Pilgrims landed at Plymouth, we were here. Before the pen of Jefferson etched across the pages of history the majestic words of the Declaration of Independence, we were here. For more than two centuries our foreparents laboured in this country without wages; they made cotton king; and they built the homes of their masters in the midst of brutal injustice and shameful humiliation – and yet out of a bottomless vitality they continued to thrive and develop.[3]

The days following the North's victory in the American Civil War had been days of hope. Successive amendments to the Constitution outlawed slavery, protected the freed slaves' social and political liberties and guaranteed the right to vote. As the old South was reconstructed fourteen blacks were elected to the House of Representatives in Washington. But resistance to equality had deep roots. In the wake of defeat whites formed the Ku Klux Klan, a terrorist organization determined to return black Americans to powerlessness through systematic intimidation and violence. Between 1889 and 1901 over two thousand blacks were lynched in the South. Racist politicians – encouraged by Northern indifference – wrote 'Jim Crow' laws into state constitutions, enforcing segregation.

Voting laws were rigged locally to crush black Southerners' potential power by denying them a political voice. States instituted unequal punishment for crimes committed by blacks and whites, excluded blacks from juries, prohibited interracial marriage and established separate schools and public facilities. The United States Supreme Court ruling on *Plessy* v *Ferguson* in 1896 underpinned the continuation of segregation into the twentieth century. Homer Plessy had refused to ride in a designated black railway carriage and was charged with violating Louisiana law requiring 'separate but equal' facilities for blacks and whites.[4] The Supreme Court upheld his conviction, institutionalizing segregation for three generations.

It is important to remember the hopelessness that first slavery and then segregation were intended to instil in black Americans, the systematic attempts to render their lives meaningless, to deny them the fruits of what claimed to be a 'land of opportunity'. But, just as the slaves had never accepted their condition passively, there was continual black resistance against the humiliation of segregation.

The National Association for the Advancement of Colored People (NAACP) was formed in 1909 to work for integration and equal opportunity for black Americans. The NAACP concentrated on legal actions against discrimination and won several significant victories. The Congress of Racial Equality (CORE), founded in 1942, favoured direct action on the model of Gandhi's passive resistance against British imperialism in India. CORE mounted a successful anti-segregation sit-in at a Chicago restaurant in 1943, a tactic taken up in other cities. Following a Supreme Court decision outlawing segregation on interstate transport CORE activists went on a 'Journey of Reconciliation' through the Southern states in 1947, testing the limits of integration.

In 1941 A. Philip Randolph, a civil rights activist and president of the Brotherhood of Sleeping Car Porters, the largest black union, had threatened to mount a 100,000-strong black march on Washington against discrimination in industry and the armed forces. President Roosevelt responded by outlawing employment discrimination in war industries and appointed a Fair Employment Practices Committee.

Black troops fought in segregated units in both world wars. In 1948 President Truman ordered the integration of the armed forces. Now black Americans prevented from eating with whites in a Mississippi restaurant could at least die alongside them in Korea.

Six years later the NAACP achieved an important victory in the Supreme Court decision *Brown* v *Board of Education of Topeka* which ruled segregation in public schools illegal and began the process of reversing *Plessy* v *Ferguson*. But much remained to be achieved. It was against this background of the historic refusal to accept both slavery and segregation that Martin Luther King's career as the voice of the civil rights campaign began.

'YOU'RE AS GOOD AS ANYONE ELSE'

Michael King (he did not officially become Martin Luther King Jr until 1934) was born, the middle of three children, on 15 January 1929 at his grandparents' two-storey Victorian frame house in Auburn Avenue, Atlanta, Georgia. The neighbourhood was marked by the symbols of the prosperity enjoyed by its successful black middle-class residents. Atlanta itself was the site of some of America's most prominent black businesses – banks, insurance companies and newspapers. The economic and cultural gap between the black professionals inhabiting Auburn Avenue and their poorer counterparts in the city's ghetto was stark. But divided as they were by income, the two groups shared the colour of their skin and could not escape the racism endemic in the Southern states.

King's father, the pastor of the Ebenezer Street Baptist Church, was an influential member of the black community. The son of a Georgia share-cropper, Martin Luther King Sr (also originally named Michael King) left home as a child to follow his sister to Atlanta, where he worked his way through high school and college. It was almost inevitable that King Sr should take one of the few routes to status open to an ambitious black American since the days of slavery, the ministry. In 1926 he married Alberta, the schoolteacher daughter of Adam Daniel Williams, founding pastor of Ebenezer Baptist Church. On Williams's death in 1931 King succeeded to the pastorship of the almost bankrupt church.

King Sr, despite the Depression, restored Ebenezer's fortunes, taking the view that financial as well as spiritual welfare was the church's concern. On racial issues King Sr was ambivalent. Though courageous in confronting segregation when touched as an individual, he preferred evasion as a tactic and avoided discussion of the issue with his family. He led a black voter registration drive in Atlanta in 1935 but abandoned a campaign for equal pay for black schoolteachers following criticism from his poorer parishioners for taking up the interests of an already privileged group.

Relatively protected though his childhood was, King Jr experienced the South's pervasive racism early in life. 'Whites only' signs made it clear that the black population, rich and poor, was to be kept in its place: there were swimming pools and playgrounds that blacks could not enter, seats in buses and cinemas in which they could not sit, restaurants and shops from which they were barred. When he was six, King's friendship with two white boys was broken by their parents. King's mother told him, 'Don't let it make you feel you're not as good as white people. You're as good as anyone else, and don't you forget it!'[1]

At the age of eight, two years after beginning his education at David T. Howard Elementary School, King found early morning work as a newspaper delivery boy. By thirteen he was the youngest assistant manager of an *Atlanta Journal* delivery station. King understood that he could never become a manager, a role restricted to whites. He used the money he earned to buy fashionable clothes (at high school his vanity would earn him the nickname 'Tweedie'). But he also bought books on black history, the resistance waged against slavery and discrimination by such figures as Nat

Turner and Denmark Vesey, Frederick Douglass and Booker T. Washington.

It was at the Booker T. Washington High School, which he entered in 1942, that King – absorbing, as the heir to two generations of ministers, the rhythms of fundamentalist preaching – developed as a speaker. At fourteen he won first prize in an oratorical competition for a speech entitled 'The Negro and the Constitution'. Working in the North as a labourer at a Connecticut tobacco farm during a summer vacation, King saw unsegregated restaurants, shops and cinemas. He felt an intense liberation, not realizing that the absence of 'White' and 'Colored' signs did not mean there was no discrimination.

King entered Morehouse College, Atlanta (where his father had gone before him), at the age of fifteen. The all-black, all-male college which King joined in September 1944 was described as 'the Negro Harvard'. But under wartime financial pressure, the college had lowered its entrance age and educational standards. At Morehouse, in an atmosphere in which it was possible for the first time to discuss segregation and how whites forced black Americans to live, King began feeling his way towards what he intended to do and, as important, the philosophy that would provide a basis for his actions.

Initially reluctant to follow his father and grandfather into the ministry, King saw his future as a lawyer or doctor. But he was impressed by Henry Thoreau's seminal *Essay on Civil Disobedience* and its argument that people should refuse to recognize laws they regarded as unjust, provided they accepted the sanctions society imposed for their transgression.

King, despite a growing freedom from the constrictions of his father's Baptist fundamentalism, began to appreciate the part religion played in black American life and the platform it offered to work for change. The churches provided a comfort for suffering (and, for this reason, could be criticized as agents for passive conformism) and a refuge from white domination. They also provided an arena for black self-organization.

Morehouse's president, Dr Benjamin E. Mays, a friend of King's father, was an influential figure in King's decision to enter the ministry. From Mays, King had his introduction to the 'social gospel', a religious practice which talked not only of the soul but sought to confront the conditions in which people lived. This promised to resolve King's doubts over Christianity's intellectual weakness and its relevance to black Americans' everyday lives.

King's talent as a speaker grew and at the age of seventeen he delivered his first public sermon. In February 1948 King was ordained a full minister and became assistant pastor to his father at Ebenezer Baptist Church, the third member of what had become a dynasty. In June he graduated as a BA in Sociology and was awarded a scholarship to Crozer Theological Seminary, Chester, Pennsylvania.

Crozer, which King entered in September 1948, provided his first experience of integrated education: a third of his class was black. Studying Christian ethics, social philosophy and the psychology of religion, King thrived intellectually, becoming first in his class and the first black to be elected president of the student body. Crozer's curriculum was wide and rigorous and King worked systematically through Aristotle, Hegel, Kant, Locke, Luther, Plato and Rousseau. His reading of Marx's *Communist Manifesto* – together with the hysterically anti-Soviet atmosphere of late 1940s America – led him to describe Communism as a 'Christian heresy' which he rejected for its ethical relativism and an apparently inherent totalitarianism. However, in an autobiographical essay in 1951 he was to write of his 'present anti-capitalist feelings'.[2]

The most profound intellectual influence on King at Crozer was Walter Rauschenbusch's *Christianity and the Social Crisis,* which had introduced the concept of the 'social gospel' to the United States. Rauschenbusch was concerned with the part Christianity could play in the quest for social justice. King described how he arrived at the conviction 'that any religion which professes to be concerned about the souls of men and is not concerned about the social and economic conditions that scar the soul is a spiritually moribund religion'.[3] But King also admired Reinhold Niebuhr, a theologian who argued that the 'social gospel' was misguided, that while individuals were capable of responding to an appeal to reason and justice, institutions and organizations were invariably amoral.

The influence of Mahatma Gandhi at this point in King's life is less clear. In 1949 Dr Mordecai Johnson, president of Washington DC's all-black Howard University, returned from India and lectured in Philadelphia on Gandhi's life and work. King later claimed that this had prompted him to read more deeply, although he was never specific. It was, perhaps, too easy for the media in the America of the 1960s to attempt to portray King as Gandhi's heir and too complex for King to deny the role.

In June 1951 King graduated from Crozer as a Bachelor of Divinity, took first prize as the most outstanding student of his year, was awarded a fellowship for graduate study and received the gift of a car from his father. In September he entered Boston University to begin studies for a doctoral thesis in Systematic Theology.

It was in Boston that King met Coretta Scott, the daughter of a prosperous merchant from Marion, Alabama. Scott was studying to be a concert singer. At first unimpressed, she warmed to King's eloquence and sincerity but was surprised on their first date to be told that she possessed all the qualities King was looking for in a wife. She had not been the first candidate for this position. The relationship developed and, despite an initial coolness between Scott and her future father-in-law, King Sr presided at the couple's marriage on the lawn of her family home in Marion on 18 June 1953. Scott insisted that the injunction to 'obey' was omitted from the marriage vow.

The couple completed their studies in 1954, though it remained for King to write up his thesis, which he did and he was awarded a doctorate in June 1955. ~~Scholars studying his writing later suggested that parts of the thesis were plagiarized.~~[4] Although considering a career in teaching (Morehouse College made it clear he was welcome), King sought a post as a preacher. Coretta, who had hoped to make a new life outside the intensely racist atmosphere of Alabama, would have preferred him to accept an offer of a parish in the North. King himself considered the opportunity to escape segregation but felt he had a duty to return to the South, at least for a few years.

King chose to take up the pastorship of Dexter Avenue Baptist Church in Montgomery, Alabama. There were attractions: not only did middle-class Dexter Avenue offer $4,200 a year (making King the highest-paid pastor in the city), but Montgomery – at the heart of the old Confederacy – provided a signal opportunity to put the social gospel into practice. Although not formally installed until October, King preached his first sermon at Dexter Avenue in May 1954.

Two weeks later the United States Supreme

Court delivered its ruling on *Brown* v *Board of Education of Topeka*, an epoch-making declaration that 'in the field of public education the doctrine of "separate but equal" has no place'. The Supreme Court condemned segregated facilities as 'inherently unequal' and issued enforcement decrees ordering compliance with the judgment 'with all deliberate speed'. The segregationist South felt threatened and reacted by forming White Citizens' Councils to resist the Supreme Court decision. Against a background of racial tension in Montgomery King was propelled into a test of his beliefs, ideas and character.

THREE

'IF WE ARE WRONG – GOD ALMIGHTY IS WRONG'

King's father had not been slow to express disappointment that his son should choose to go to Montgomery rather than take his position as heir apparent to the church in Ebenezer Street. King was determined that his future would be in his own hands. 'I'm going to run that church,' he told his wife before taking up the post at Dexter Avenue. But King Sr's influence remained strong and the new pastor followed his father's model in centralizing control and reorganizing the church's finances.

In July 1955, (less than a year after his appointment King) apparently dissatisfied with Dexter's limitations, considered the offer of a post at Dillard

University, New Orleans, one involving both teaching and preaching. He was, however, building connections in Montgomery. <u>King joined the Montgomery branch of the National Association for the Advancement of Colored People (NAACP)</u>, accepting a place on the executive committee, and contemplated standing for election to its presidency. He also built a lasting friendship with the Revd Ralph Abernathy, pastor of the First Baptist Church and the man who was to become one of King's closest colleagues in the civil rights movement.

King's arrival in Montgomery coincided with increasing black resentment over segregation on the city's buses. Over three-quarters of the passengers were black students, workers and domestic servants, yet the front seats were reserved for whites while black passengers were forced to the back and expected to stand if white places were full. The bus drivers, who were all white, were notorious for their racial abuse and invariably called black men, whatever their age, 'Boy'. In March 1955 a fifteen-year-old high school student, Claudette Colvin, refused to give up her seat to a white passenger. She was arrested, handcuffed and taken to the police station where she was charged with assault.

King was drafted on to a committee formed to protest to the city's police commissioner. The commissioner's offer of a compromise — buses would be filled on a first-come first-served basis, with black passengers filling seats from the back and whites from the front, and drivers would be instructed to be polite to all passengers — was accepted by the committee but rejected by the bus company's lawyer. He was unwilling to risk action being taken against the bus owners for contravening segregation laws. What had begun as individual action was now to take an organized form, a boycott.

A boycott of transportation by black passengers was not a new tactic. Between 1900 and 1906 boycotts had occurred in over twenty-five Southern cities. In Montgomery itself an action mounted from 1900 to 1902 temporarily ended segregation on the city's buses, only for the practice to be reinstated by local ordinances. In March 1953 a ten-day mass boycott of the transport system in Baton Rouge, Louisiana, led by the Revd Theodore J. Jemison, a former NAACP branch president, culminated in a compromise. Similar actions followed in New Orleans and in Tallahassee, Florida. It was on these examples that Montgomery built.

King was for the moment preoccupied by more domestic concerns. The Kings' first child was born on 17 November 1955. She was named, at his wife's insistence and against King's objection to what he felt was unnecessary ornateness, Yolanda Denise.

Two weeks later, on 1 December, Rosa Parks, a 42-year-old seamstress and secretary of the Montgomery NAACP, refused to give up her seat on a bus to a white passenger, was arrested and charged with violation of the segregation laws. She was bailed out by E.D. Nixon and a white liberal sympathizer. Nixon chaired the local NAACP and was a union activist. Parks accepted Nixon's suggestion that she should act as a test case against segregation. This was to be combined with a black boycott of the city's buses.

Planning by Montgomery's black movements, including the NAACP and the Women's Political Council (an organization of professional women), began at once. To ensure the widest possible support Nixon telephoned the city's preachers. King, third on his list, asked for time to consider Nixon's proposal, but agreed to the Dexter Avenue Church being used for a meeting of the city's black leaders. Abernathy persuaded King to support the action.

The fifty-strong meeting held in the church basement decided to call for a one-day bus boycott on Monday 5 December, the day Parks was to appear in court. The organizers demanded seating on a first-come first-served basis, an end to racist abuse from drivers, and the recruitment of black drivers – a moderation rather than an end to segregation. 'We ask only', King was to write, 'for what in Atlanta, Mobile, Charleston and most other cities of the South is considered the southern pattern.'[1]

On the Monday morning King and his wife watched from their window, waiting for the first bus to pass. It was empty, as were those that followed. King drove around the city to see that later buses carried few passengers, all white. Over 17,500 black people were supporting the action. In court Parks was fined $10. The bus operators' refusal to meet the protesters' modest demands transformed a one-day boycott into a year-long struggle to remove segregation entirely.

At a meeting in the afternoon the boycott leaders formed a Montgomery Improvement Association (MIA), appointing King as president. As a new-comer to Montgomery King's asset was his distance from the factionalism among those attempting to cooperate in organizing the campaign. But his speech to a mass meeting at Holt Street Baptist Church that evening – his first political address – demonstrated that the movement had found its voice. King had little time to write more than odd notes for the speech, but as he spoke it appeared that his life had been a preparation for the moment. He condemned violence and declared that the boycotters were asking simply for their rights as American citizens:

> We are not wrong in what we are doing. If we are wrong – the Supreme Court of this nation is wrong. If we are wrong – God Almighty is wrong!'[2]

King was twenty-six years old and his rise to prominence had begun.

Practical problems of continuing the boycott remained. Black taxi drivers had initially agreed to carry passengers for a flat 10 cents but were restrained by the city's fare regulations. King contacted Jemison, the organizer of the 1953 Baton Rouge boycott and now secretary of the National Baptist Convention, for advice on organizing what would prove to be an effective car pool. The pool had the paradoxical effect not only of drawing the classes among blacks together – with more prosperous car owners ferrying the poor – but also, in some cases, the races, as white female employers picked up their black servants and drove them to and from work.

By early 1956 the city's store owners were reporting $1 million in lost sales and the bus company was suffering a 65 per cent drop in income. In response the city police harassed boycotters, arresting them for 'loitering' as they waited for cars, and drivers, who were charged with often spurious traffic offences.

On 26 January King himself was arrested – the first of 120 arrests he would experience over the next twelve years – and jailed for exceeding the speed limit by 5 mph. As he was driven to the prison outside Montgomery rather than to the police station, King feared he was about to be lynched. However, following a demonstration led by Abernathy, he was released on bail. The experience, which followed shortly after a telephoned death threat, and combined with the pressures of his position at the centre of the boycott, brought King to his lowest ebb. He wrote later of sitting alone in his kitchen feeling that he could not continue. Finally an inner voice reassured him and his fears evaporated.

However, the pressures did not abate. As the MIA executive committee agreed on 30 January to proceed with a federal suit against bus segregation and to continue the boycott, King was told that a bomb had exploded at his home. Neither his wife nor daughter had been injured, but an angry crowd – some armed with knives and guns – gathered outside the house. King urged the crowd to disperse and to reject violence, calling on them to meet hate with love. He rejected appeals from his father and father-in-law to leave Montgomery for his own safety.

King continued the theme of reconciliation at a mass rally a few days later:

> This is not a war between the white and the Negro but a conflict between justice and injustice,' he declared. 'We are not just trying to improve the Negro of Montgomery but the whole of Montgomery.[3]

Here, in a few words, was King's talent: the attempt to secure the redress of black grievances by appealing to a shared concept of justice that would draw the races in America together. However, on a practical level King felt continuing doubts. He told the black singer and prominent civil rights activist Harry Belafonte, 'I need your help. I have no idea where this movement is going.'[4]

In March an all-white jury found King and eighty-eight other boycott organizers guilty of violating a statute prohibiting 'interference with a business'. King was fined $500, with the alternative of 386 days' hard labour. The conviction was overturned when a federal court ruled in May that bus segregation in Montgomery was unconstitutional. The city authorities appealed against the decision to the Supreme Court and the boycott continued.

Unofficial action against the boycotters was stepped up. The 12,000-strong White Citizens' Council (which included the mayor and the entire City Commission among its membership) issued leaflets threatening violence against Montgomery's black population. An attempt to sue King for $15,000 damages collapsed in November when the Supreme Court confirmed the unconstitutionality of bus segregation. Ku Klux Klan intimidation –

forty carloads drove through the black neighbourhood in white robes – foundered as it was treated
with contempt.

On 21 December King, accompanied by
Abernathy, Nixon and Glenn Smiley, a white
minister, rode on Montgomery's first desegregated
bus. Less prominent individuals continued to suffer
as whites attacked buses with stones and, on a
number of occasions, gunfire. Two black homes,
including Abernathy's, and four black churches were
bombed in a wave of white extremist rage. In
January 1957 sticks of dynamite planted on King's
front porch failed to explode.

It was the persistence of Montgomery's black
population that made the boycott effective. King
was the inspirational figurehead who won national
and international attention for their action. But the
bus boycott – mass action combined with the
NAACP's classical strategy of using the courts –
represented a success in only one area. Segregation
in Montgomery continued in education (in
February 1956 white students at the University of
Alabama rioted to prevent the enrolment of a
black student), hotels, restaurants and in
employment.

The boycott had, however, signalled to black people throughout America that they could achieve change through direct action and had made King an international figure. What was necessary for further advance was a movement that could organize effectively across the Southern states.

'GIVE US THE BALLOT'

Following the Montgomery events King faced two crucial questions: could the success be built upon and what was his future role? In the bus boycott black people had protested by withdrawing from a facility already open to them. To overturn discrimination in areas to which they had no access would involve confrontation, leading to arrests, injuries and – given the South's history of violence towards black people – deaths.

King had proved himself to be an inspirational speaker and a consistent advocate of non-violence. He had rejected black triumphalism, together with the separatism of the Northern-based Nation of Islam, urging integration based on Christian (and American) values. Although much of the day-to-day organization of the Montgomery boycott had been the responsibility of others, King's effectiveness as a figurehead had drawn the action to world attention, making him an internationally recognized figure.

Unsure of the next stage, King, still carrying his responsibilities as Dexter Avenue's minister, concentrated on public speaking and fund-raising, with never fewer than four engagements a week outside Montgomery. He remained a compelling orator, fierce in his denunciations of discrimination, eloquent in his calls for reconciliation, but segregation remained as firmly entrenched as ever throughout the South. Was oratory – however satisfying to the audience and, for the moment, to King himself – enough?

Many whites remained adamant in their opposition to King's message and to the Supreme Court's ruling against segregated public schooling. Over ninety Southern politicians signed a manifesto advocating resistance to integration by 'every lawful means'. Not all their followers confined themselves to legal methods.

King, acting on a suggestion from Bayard Rustin (a leader of the pacifist Fellowship of Reconciliation and a former Communist who had helped in the Montgomery campaign), called black church leaders together in Atlanta, Georgia, on 9 January

1957. The meeting established the Southern Christian Leadership Conference (SCLC) to co-ordinate local civil rights activities through black churches. As in Montgomery, the SCLC would encourage a 'spiritual strategy' running parallel with the NAACP's pressure through the courts. King was elected president, a position he retained until his death.

The Atlanta meeting called on President Eisenhower to come South to order whites to abide by Supreme Court decisions on segregation. The SCLC's second meeting in New Orleans on 14 February 1957 asked the President to call a White House conference on civil rights. The SCLC declared that if he failed to do this, it would organize a Prayer Pilgrimage in Washington to draw attention to the violence black people were suffering. Eisenhower dismissed the SCLC proposal.

The message to Eisenhower had been drafted by Rustin and Stanley Levison, a white civil liberties activist with Communist connections to whom King had been introduced by Rustin. Levison, a socialist who had prospered through real estate investment, had supported the Communist Party financially during the McCarthyite persecutions of the early

1950s. King, although rejecting Marxism as an ideology, acknowledged the largely creditable record of the party over race issues.

Levison became a colleague in the civil rights struggle for the remainder of King's life, and a close friend. But the connection, together with King's growing prominence, attracted the attention of Federal Bureau of Investigation (FBI) director, J. Edgar Hoover, a virulent anti-Communist with little sympathy for black activism. Hoover ordered that King be placed under surveillance as a 'Communist' and initiated an operation to undermine civil rights groups.

The FBI had mounted similar operations in the past against black activists W.E.B. Du Bois and Marcus Garvey, singer Paul Robeson and writer James Baldwin. In King's case, Hoover feared that he might succeed in welding the fragmented black factions together nationally as effectively as he had in Montgomery. Equally alarming to Hoover was a socialist tendency, at least in American establishment terms, in King's thinking. King pointed to aspirations shared by black and white workers for a fairer share in what they produced, for security in their old age and when they were sick or unemployed. The FBI would insist in briefings to successive presidents and the media that King was under Communist influence.

The approach to President Eisenhower gained King further publicity. *Time* magazine featured King on its cover, describing him as 'the scholarly Negro Baptist minister who in little more than a year has risen from nowhere to become one of the nation's remarkable leaders of men'. *Time* praised King for reaching:

> beyond the law books and writs, beyond violence and threats, to win his people – and challenge all people – with a spiritual force that aspires even to ending prejudice in men's minds.[1]

In March, President Kwame Nkrumah of newly independent Ghana invited King, together with NAACP executive secretary Roy Wilkins, A. Philip Randolph, head of the Brotherhood of Sleeping Car Porters, Ralph Bunche and Adam Clayton Powell, to celebrate the west African state's freedom from Britain. The impact on black America of the European powers' rapid withdrawal from their African colonies was profound.

On their return King, Wilkins and Randolph concentrated on the Prayer Pilgrimage, with Levison's multiracial organization In Friendship providing finance. On 17 May 1957 – the third anniversary of the Supreme Court's ruling on educational desegregation – 37,000 demonstrators gathered at the Lincoln Memorial in Washington, the largest civil rights rally yet mounted. Speakers included the black entertainers Sammy Davis Jr, Sidney Poitier and Harry Belafonte.

King, making his first national address, denounced the 'silent and apathetic' attitude of Congress and the White House to civil rights and the federal government's failure to enforce black voting rights in the South. 'Give us the ballot, and we will no longer have to worry the federal government about our basic rights,' King declared. He continued the theme of mutual respect. 'We must act in such a way as to make possible a coming-together of white people and colored people on the basis of a real harmony of interests and understanding.'[2]

Shortly after the Washington Pilgrimage King became the youngest recipient of the NAACP's Springam Medal for his contribution to race relations. But on 3 September he was charged with loitering while accompanying Abernathy to court in Montgomery and fined $10. King refused to pay and the costs were met by the police commissioner, who accused King of seeking publicity. Abernathy had attended court for the trial of a man accused of attacking him and, in the course of the hearing, there were allegations of Abernathy's involvement in an extramarital affair. King was to face similar accusations in the future.

A week later a Civil Rights Act, pushed through Congress by Southern Democrat Senator Lyndon B. Johnson, established a Civil Rights Commission and a Civil Rights Division in the Justice Department. But the Supreme Court's injunction 'with all deliberate speed' was having to be fought school by school and college by college. At the end of September President Eisenhower deployed federal troops to escort nine black children into an all-white high school at Little Rock, Arkansas. The moderation of the Civil Rights Act disappointed the SCLC. King saw that outside pressure remained essential. He argued that black Americans should take direct action themselves without waiting for government support or a court order.

King presented the SCLC with his proposals for a 'Crusade for Citizenship' on 18 October. The goal was to register two million black voters before the 1960 presidential elections. Southern states disenfranchised black citizens through poll taxes, literacy tests which discriminated in favour of whites, and intimidation of individuals able to surmount these obstacles. So effective were they that in King's own Montgomery County, of nearly thirty thousand blacks of voting age only two thousand were on the register.

King's projected Crusade – mass meetings, appeals to blacks to register, with support from local committees – was over ambitious. At this stage the SCLC was in reality little more than a gathering of preachers prone to verbose speeches and procrastination. To be effective the campaign needed the cooperation of local chapters of the NAACP, which was planning its own voter registration drive and resented competition.

King, meanwhile, maintained a punishing schedule of public speaking and fund-raising. In addition he was producing his personal account (with help from a ghost writer) of the Montgomery boycott, *Stride Toward Freedom*. On 23 October his wife gave birth to their second child, Martin Luther King III.

As it became clear that the Crusade's organization was faltering, a disappointed King launched a bitter attack on the black poor at a Montgomery conference in December. Reciting statistics on black crime rates and illegitimacy, he said that oppression was no excuse. He then turned on the black middle class, denouncing an academic fraternity that spent more annually on alcohol than the NAACP's entire budget. The appointment of veteran black activist Ella Baker as Crusade organizer – despite King's initial objection that she was a woman and not a preacher – provided a last-minute impetus. On 12 February 1958 – the birthday of Abraham Lincoln, the emancipator of the slaves – rallies in twenty-one Southern cities, though enthusiastically attended, had little direct impact. However, in June President Eisenhower agreed at a White House meeting with King, Randolph and Wilkins on the need for firmer legislation to protect black voting rights.

King's activity now came to a dramatic halt. Signing copies of *Stride Toward Freedom* in a Harlem shop in September, King was stabbed by a mentally ill black woman. The weapon, a letter opener, lodged between his heart and lung. A doctor later told King that had he sneezed while waiting for surgery he would have drowned in his own blood.

A long convalescence gave King the opportunity in February 1959 to accept an invitation from the Gandhi Peace Foundation to visit India. One writer has noted, bluntly but not inaccurately, that King 'wanted time to absorb Gandhism as a discipline that might help him escape a drift toward stagnation as a glorified after-dinner speaker'.[3]

King's tour included a four-hour discussion with the Indian prime minister, Jawaharlal Nehru, who felt the need to remind an over-idealistic King of Gandhi's 'pragmatism'. King also met Indians who had known Gandhi. He later wrote:

> I left India more convinced than ever before that non-violent resistance is the most potent weapon available to oppressed people in their struggle for freedom.[4]

But King returned in the spring to find violence raging in the South – a white mob lynched a young black man in Mississippi – and a disorganized SCLC.

At the movement's convention King admitted that the 'Crusade for Citizenship' had failed, while the NAACP's campaign for voter registration was flourishing. He blamed SCLC executive director John Tilley and demanded his resignation. Tilley was replaced by Ella Baker. King also acknowledged the impossibility of combining a full-time ministry at Dexter Avenue with his campaigning work. In November 1959 he announced he would move to Atlanta, where the SCLC had established its headquarters, and return to his former role as assistant pastor to his father at Ebenezer Street.

King conducted his last service at Dexter on 31 January 1960. The following day black students in North Carolina opened a new front in the struggle for equality. In the six years since the Supreme Court ruling on ending segregated education, only 4 per cent of black students had been admitted to white schools. Congress and the White House seemed paralysed as the presidential elections approached, with even liberals afraid of the effect on their white constituents of appearing friendly to black rights. King's organization, the SCLC, had failed to build on the Montgomery success while the NAACP appeared to be making little progress in the legal field. More radical action was necessary.

On 1 February four students, all NAACP Youth Council members, asked to be served at a segregated Woolworth's lunch counter in Greensboro, North Carolina. When they were refused they stayed in their seats. The next day they were joined by twenty more students and then by over a hundred, including whites from the University of North Carolina Women's College. By mid-April, sit-ins had spread spontaneously to over seventy-five Southern cities, with fifty thousand black students and white sympathizers active in the campaign. The protesters faced assault and arrest. Although King had not initiated the campaign, participants took his non-violent philosophy as an inspiration. Indeed one of the students on the 1 February sit-in had been reading a comic book entitled *Martin Luther King and the Montgomery Story* the day before. King, with his invariable magnanimity, was unstinting in his praise for the students' courage.

Mass action guaranteed television coverage, encouraging further support. 'We Shall Overcome', which the students sang as they were arrested, was adopted as the civil rights anthem. In the Northern states demonstrators picketed stores owned by chains known to discriminate in the South. For King it was clear that the sit-ins represented a practical application of his philosophy of non-violent direct action. In June 1961 he declared that the demonstrators had succeeded in forcing integration of lunch counters in 142 Southern cities, 'without a single court suit . . . without spending millions and millions of dollars'.[5]

At the end of April over a hundred of the leading activists established the Student Nonviolent Coordinating Committee (SNCC) in Raleigh, North Carolina. Although the meeting was convened by the SCLC's Ella Baker the students rejected King's appeal for the new movement to affiliate to the SCLC; however, they accepted financial help from his organization.

On 19 October King joined a sit-in at Atlanta's main department store at the request of the students. His almost inevitable arrest drew him into Democratic presidential candidate John F. Kennedy's campaign and began a relationship with the Kennedys that was to prove both difficult and useful. King was sentenced to four months' hard labour at a Georgia work camp for violating probation on a previous minor traffic charge. The harsh sentence shocked many people and there were fears that King's life was in danger. Kennedy, acting on a suggestion from his aides, telephoned King's wife to express his concern. His brother Robert, at first angry at the call which he said would lose Kennedy three Southern states if it became public, then telephoned the judge involved and persuaded him to release King pending appeal.

Members of the election campaign team saw the advantage of using the Kennedy calls to win black votes. Without informing either of the brothers they produced and distributed two million pamphlets containing pro-Kennedy statements at black churches. Care was taken to ensure minimal publicity in the mainstream press to avoid alienating white voters in the South.

King's father declared that although he had not intended to support Kennedy, because he was a Catholic, he would now vote for him. King himself, though holding back from endorsing Kennedy, publicly credited the presidential candidate with his release. From being the least popular candidate with the black electorate Kennedy won an estimated three-quarters of the black vote in November, giving him, black leaders claimed, the edge in his narrow victory over Nixon. King, the movement's acknowledged inspiration, was not invited to Kennedy's inauguration in January 1961.

Many activists understood that Kennedy's attachment to civil rights was largely a tactic to win Northern black votes. He had, for example, criticized Eisenhower's use of federal troops to assist desegregation in 1957. But could these votes now be used to push the White House into action? In the weeks before Kennedy's inauguration the Supreme Court, adding to a previous ruling made in the 1940s, declared the segregation of passengers on interstate buses, trains and in terminals unconstitutional. Would the new administration enforce the ruling in the South?

'THEY DON'T UNDERSTAND WHAT WE'RE DOING'

King and his fellow civil rights leaders were soon disappointed with the new administration. Black interests were low on the Kennedy agenda, not least because of the President's political dependence on white Southern Democrats, the 'Dixiecrats'. An early Kennedy act was to appoint three virulent segregationists – one of whom described black people as 'monkeys' – to federal judgeships in the South.

In 1961 President Kennedy rejected proposals from King and NAACP leader Wilkins to end discrimination in the federal civil service by executive order. He refused to force federal contractors to introduce equal opportunities programmes or to write non-discrimination clauses into federally funded programmes. The administration did, however, set up an advisory Committee on Equal Employment Opportunity, chaired by Vice-President Johnson.

But, before it became clear that the Kennedy presidency represented the triumph of style over content, liberal young Americans were galvanized by his inaugural message, 'Ask not what your country can do for you – ask what you can do for your country.' The more determined of them, black *and* white, went into the heart of the segregated South on Freedom Rides. Building on the experience of similar actions in the 1940s the Freedom Riders confronted segregation on interstate buses and in terminals, both ruled unconstitutional by the Supreme Court.

The Freedom Rides were directed by James Farmer, head of the Congress of Racial Equality (CORE), which had been organizing non-violent direct action since its foundation in 1942. The riders themselves were volunteers from CORE and the Student Nonviolent Coordinating Committee (SNCC). Farmer had a clear strategy. White racists were to be provoked into revealing the reality of segregation. 'We figured that the government would have to respond if we created a situation that was headline news all over the world, and affected the nation's image abroad.'[1] President Kennedy's imminent departure for a summit meeting with Soviet leader Khruschev in Vienna added to the propaganda potential. As with the 1960 sit-ins King took no direct part in the initiation or organization of the Freedom Rides. But he was to play a crucial part at a dramatic moment of the action, using the influential position he had acquired since the Montgomery boycott .

Two scheduled buses left Washington on 4 May 1961 carrying four black and four white Freedom Riders together with a CORE observer. The plan was to travel through Virginia, North and South Carolina, Alabama and Mississippi, desegregating bus terminal waiting rooms and lunch counters by the simple, but dangerous, process of using them. The initial reception was hostile, but not violent, and they successfully integrated facilities in Virginia and North Carolina. But when the first bus pulled into Rock Hill, South Carolina, the riders were brutally attacked by whites in a terminal waiting room, while local police stood outside.

The second bus reached Anniston, Alabama (an area in which the Ku Klux Klan was strongly organized) on 14 May. A white mob armed with iron bars, pistols and knives smashed the bus windows and slashed its tyres. A few hours later, having left the town, the bus was firebombed. Freedom Riders attempting to escape the flames and smoke were beaten by the attackers. In Birmingham their fellow riders were ambushed by Klan members.

Unable to find a driver willing to face further attacks CORE temporarily abandoned the rides. But a few days later another bus set out from Nashville, Tennessee, financed by the local SCLC. The riders were arrested as they entered Birmingham and dumped in the middle of the night on the border with Tennessee. They returned to Birmingham and set out for Montgomery, the scene of the 1955–6 bus boycott. At the Montgomery terminal the riders were attacked by whites wielding baseball bats and iron bars and all twenty-two were injured, some seriously. Although there were no police at the terminal – and FBI agents on the scene confined themselves to making notes – there were television cameras and a photographer from *Life* magazine. The viciousness of the white response was immediately exposed throughout America and beyond.

King and Abernathy, in Chicago on a speaking engagement, hurried to Montgomery, where King expressed his support for the Freedom Riders. He called a meeting at Abernathy's First Baptist Church to rally local support for the campaign. On 21 May as the thousand-strong congregation gathered together with the Freedom Riders, a white mob massed outside. When King arrived the crowd began throwing stones through the church's stained-glass windows and set fire to cars in the street.

A month before, King had an unpublicized meeting with Attorney General Robert Kennedy. He was accompanied, to Kennedy's amusement, by Levison, whose telephone was being tapped by the FBI. Using this contact, King called Kennedy and asked for protection. Kennedy – alarmed by the embarrassment the scenes were causing to the administration – promised to dispatch a force of marshals. After reassuring the meeting, King and Abernathy discussed their next move. King courageously, given the temper of the crowd, insisted he should address the whites outside. The mob was unwilling to listen and King, hit by a tear gas canister, was forced to retreat into the church. As Kennedy had promised, six hundred marshals arrived and dispersed the crowd by firing volleys of tear gas. In the church King criticized Alabama governor Patterson for his failure to act. Patterson in his turn called for King to leave Montgomery, accusing him of being 'a menace to the people of this city'.[2]

King spent that evening with the Freedom Riders, CORE director Farmer and the newly appointed SCLC executive director, Wyatt Walker. The riders appealed to King to join them on the next stage. Walker tried to ward off what appeared to be criticism by explaining that King was more valuable to them conducting negotiations and fund-raising, activities difficult to undertake sitting on a bus. When the riders pressed King again, Walker said that King would face certain arrest and imprisonment. Then King intervened. 'I think,' he said, 'I should choose the time and place of my Golgotha.' Some of the riders were shocked by King's self-identification with Christ and the crucifixion.[3] King did, however, agree to become chairman of a Freedom Riders Co-ordinating Committee and to organize training in non-violence for the growing numbers of students volunteering to participate in the action. At the last of the training sessions King said that participants 'must develop the quiet courage of dying for a cause'.[4]

After the bus had left on the next leg of the journey to Jackson, Mississippi, King spoke to Robert Kennedy but was disappointed with his appeal for a 'cooling off' period. 'You know,' King complained after the conversation, 'they don't understand the social revolution going on in the world, and therefore they don't understand what we're doing.'[5]

The rides continued through the summer. In Jackson 328 Freedom Riders were arrested and imprisoned, among them Abernathy, Farmer and King's brother. Of those arrested, over half were black and a quarter women. In June King was arranging with his old college, Morehouse, to deliver a series of lectures on philosophy for a fee of $1,500. August he spent vacationing with his family at the exclusive Martha's Vineyard in a cottage rented by Levison.

However, King's negotiations on behalf of the Freedom Riders continued. Attorney General Kennedy – acting on a suggestion from King –

Martin Luther King Jr (1929–68), photographed in 1965.
(Hulton Getty Picture Library)

King, his wife Coretta, and their first child, Yolanda, outside the Dexter Avenue Baptist Church, Montgomery, Alabama, where King was pastor from 1954 to 1960. As president of the Montgomery Improvement Association, King led the successful 1955–6 bus boycott which brought him to prominence as a civil rights leader. (Dan Weiner/Magnum, detail)

A National Guard detachment protects one of the buses in which the Freedom Riders campaigned against Southern segregation in 1961. King chaired the Freedom Riders Co-ordinating Committee and was attacked by a white mob at a rally in the riders' support in Montgomery in May 1961. (Bruce Davidson/Magnum, detail)

King being interviewed at the Lincoln Memorial during the August 1963 March on Washington for Jobs and Freedom. The march was organized by the main civil rights organizations – King's Southern Christian Leadership Conference (SCLC), the National Association for the Advancement of Colored People (NAACP) and the Congress of Racial Equality (CORE) – and was supported by a number of white churches and trade unions. (Hulton Getty Picture Library)

King greets the 250,000-strong August 1963 March on Washington. At the rally King made his celebrated 'I have a dream' speech in which he looked to the day 'when all God's children, black men and white men, Jews and Gentiles, Protestants and Catholics, will be able to join hands and sing in the words of the old Negro spiritual, "Free at last, free at last, thank God Almighty, we're free at last".' (Hulton Getty Picture Library)

King at a meeting with President Lyndon Johnson in the White House in 1965. Johnson was a committed supporter of black rights and invited King to be present at the signing of the Civil Rights Act in July 1964 and of the Voting Rights Act in August 1965. Relations between the two were soured by the escalating war in Vietnam.
(Hulton Getty Picture Library)

King and his wife Coretta lead the final leg of the March 1965 Selma– Montgomery march to the Capitol Building. King told a 25,000-strong crowd, 'We are on the move now. Like and idea whose time has come, not even the marching of mighty armies can halt us.' Anger at white violence during the march strengthened President Johnson's promotion of the Voting Rights Act. (Hulton Getty Picture Library, detail)

King addresses supporters outside Antioch Baptist Church during a voter registration drive conducted in the South in 1966 following the 1965 Voting Rights Act. During the campaign the slogan 'Black Power' was first used and King's encouragement of non-violence and cooperation with white liberals was criticized by black militants.

(Bob Adelman / Magnum, detail)

Blacks and whites demonstrate their support for King's message as his body is taken through the streets of Atlanta, from Ebenezer Baptist Church (where he had been ordained in 1948) to Morehouse College (which he attended from 1944–8), before his burial. Members of the Kennedy family were among the mourners at Ebenezer.

(Hulton Getty Picture Library)

King's widow, Coretta, and their children beside his coffin as it lies in state at Ebenezer Baptist Church, Atlanta, before King's burial beside his grandparents at the all-black South View Cemetery. The day of his burial was proclaimed a National Day of Mourning. (Constantine Manos/Magnum)

asked the Interstate Commerce Commission (ICC) to issue regulations banning segregation in interstate travel. This would strengthen the federal government's powers to enforce the Supreme Court rulings. The ICC's regulations came into effect in November and within a year CORE declared that the Freedom Riders had achieved their aims. Successful as this phase of activity had been – King was to call the Freedom Rides a psychological turning point in the civil rights campaign – the pressures on King as the movement's figurehead were mounting.

Since the Montgomery boycott King had faced constant death threats. An FBI memorandum in July 1961 reported on a Ku Klux Klan meeting in Anniston (where the Freedom Riders' bus had been firebombed) at which a Klan leader called for King to be killed, 'even if someone has to go to prison'.[6] FBI files recorded many similar threats. The FBI itself, alleging that Communists at least influenced, if they did not control, the civil rights movement, was also putting pressure on King. Attorney General Kennedy had authorized the tapping of Levison's telephone and the burglary of his office. The FBI leaked to the *New York Times*, which had been

sympathetic to black rights, a report of a conversation in which Levison had warned King that a
member of his SCLC staff was a Communist.
Embarrassed, King reluctantly dismissed the staff
member.

Divisions within the movement were a further
drain on King's energy. Roy Wilkins, executive
director of the long-established NAACP, resented
King's growing prominence as a relative newcomer.
At the other extreme the young radicals of the
SNCC (some of whom, in response to King's often
pompous public manner, nicknamed him 'De
Lawd') felt that while they were risking injury and
prison King and the SCLC were reaping the benefits
in publicity and finance. This was unfair, at least as
far as money was concerned, as the SCLC was being
pressed to meet legal costs arising from the
Freedom Rides. Finally, King's activities had
brought him into conflict with the black Baptist
Convention, of which he was vice-president. While
King had welcomed the 1960 sit-ins the Convention's
president, the Revd Joseph Jackson, had dissociated
the church from them. When a King supporter
challenged Jackson for the presidency Jackson
triumphed and King lost his foothold in the

Convention's hierarchy. The black Baptists were now divided and the Convention came out as a vigorous critic of the SCLC.

King now suffered one of his most stunning setbacks. In Albany, Georgia, he was outmanoeuvred by the police and city authorities, ignored by the Kennedy administration and, perhaps more significant, confronted with the dangers of believing the myth of omnipotence constructed around him. Albany, with a black population of 23,000 and 33,000 whites, was a rigidly segregated city. In mid-1961 SNCC activists began a voter registration project in the area, ignoring the older NAACP-oriented black leadership. Following protests against the arrest of ten Freedom Riders in December 1961 the project was broadened into an 'Albany Movement', aimed at total desegregation of the city. When a march ended with over five hundred arrests the organizers sought more experienced help.

Factional arguments over whether to call in NAACP leader Wilkins or King symbolized divisions within the movement over objectives and tactics. While the NAACP had historically favoured working through the courts, King advocated non-violent direct action in the streets. When King arrived with Abernathy on 11 December there was no overall strategy and no precise demands. King called a church meeting at which he said, 'We will wear them down by our capacity to suffer.'[7]

On 16 December King led 250 marchers singing 'We Shall Overcome' to the city hall. They were confronted by a hundred police officers commanded by police chief Laurie Pritchett. Pritchett had learnt the lesson of previous clashes in Alabama: violence attracted publicity and federal intervention. He banned the use of clubs or dogs, ordering his officers to act politely and to arrest protesters with minimum force. As civil rights activists depended on exposing the violence inherent in segregation, Pritchett's tactics effectively undermined their agitation. Ordered by Pritchett to disperse the demonstration King refused and he and his supporters were arrested for parading illegally. King vowed to remain in prison until Albany desegregated but the city commissioners outflanked him. They promised to release all the protestors, desegregate bus and rail terminals (something the ICC's regulations already obliged them to do), and to appoint a bi-racial commission to examine the

city's segregation policies. In return King was to
leave Albany and there were to be no more mass
demonstrations. King agreed and, following a sixty-
day postponement of his trial, was freed on bail on
18 December. He said on his release that Albany's
offer made it unnecessary to remain in prison. As
the city authorities delayed, preventing the
desegregation of, for example, parks and libraries
by closing them, King realized his mistake. 'We
thought the victory had been won,' he later said.
'When we got out, we discovered it was all a
hoax.'[8]

With King out of Albany, and with him the
national media, the city commissioners refused any
further negotiation. The SNCC-led movement
struggled to regain momentum by organizing sit-
ins, picketing of shops to persuade them to employ
black workers, and a bus boycott. The bus company
agreed to desegregate, but then went out of
business. The federal government made no move to
enforce black rights in the city.

King returned to Albany at the end of February
and was arrested while leading a march. On his
release he continued with his exhausting round of
public speaking and with a voter registration drive

funded by the privately financed Voter Education Project. In July he was again in Albany with Abernathy to receive the delayed sentence for their arrests in December 1961. King and Abernathy refused to pay a $198 fine and opted for forty-five days in jail. With King in Albany, media interest revived.

It was, as King realized, all too easy to be provoked into responding to violence or to give way to frustration. Training in non-violence was intended to provide a philosophical and practical grounding in resisting this. But as marches resumed, black youths stoned Albany police cars.

Released from prison, King was arrested again for leading a prayer vigil at City Hall. He declared that he would stay inside but the city authorities arranged for his fine to be paid. The city commissioners now raised the stakes by obtaining a federal court order banning King and other leaders from organizing demonstrations. The injunction put King in a difficult position and he hesitated. If he insisted on marching he would be arrested for contempt of court rather than confronting segregation, weakening the moral impact. Attorney General Kennedy, whom he telephoned to ask for the injunction to be overturned, told him it would be helpful to 'close up' action in Albany. Kennedy hoped the administration could be shielded from controversy by treating segregation as a local problem to be resolved by local negotiations.

King appeared to acquiesce. When a crowd waiting for King to take the lead marched without him at the head, he comforted himself with the declaration, 'They can stop the leaders, but they can't stop the people.'[9] That evening he faced a difficult session with SNCC activists who, though for the moment remaining committed to non-violence, vented their frustration by criticizing King's tactics. In August a pregnant black woman suffered a miscarriage after a brutal beating at a jail outside Albany. King's strategy of non-violence was again undermined as protesting black youths hurled bricks and bottles at police. King criticized the rioters and called for a day of penance, angering black supporters who would have preferred him to concentrate his condemnation on those responsible for the beating.

King left Albany at the end of August, though anti-segregation activity continued in the city for years to come. Andrew Young, an SCLC activist who later became executive director, said that the Albany debacle resulted from a 'miscalculation on the part of a number of people that a spontaneous appearance by Martin Luther King could bring change . . .'.[10] King left Albany depressed, realizing perhaps that he had fallen into the same trap. In the past – the Montgomery bus boycott, the sit-ins, the Freedom Riders, and now Albany – King had been drawn into popular and almost spontaneous actions over which he had no real control. As attention moved to Birmingham, Alabama, he was determined to take command and allow no repetition of Albany. If non-violent direct action failed in Birmingham, King's influence – and his career – might be over.

'DON'T EVEN BE AFRAID TO DIE'

The date 1 January 1963 marked the 100th anniversary of Lincoln's Emancipation Proclamation freeing the slaves. King, along with many civil rights activists, found little to celebrate. Black Americans were twice as likely as whites to be unemployed, those who had jobs were confined largely to unskilled and semi-skilled work and incomes half those of whites. Nine years after the Supreme Court had made its ruling desegregating education, under 10 per cent of Southern black students attended integrated schools.

In October 1962 King had asked President Kennedy to issue a second Emancipation Proclamation to ban segregation, presenting him with a draft. The suggestion was politely received, and ignored. King, with veteran black activist A. Philip Randolph, declined President Kennedy's invitation to a White House commemoration of Lincoln's birthday on 12 February 1963 in protest against the administration's continuing timidity over civil rights. Kennedy, stung by growing restiveness among black leaders (the NAACP was rumoured to be shifting its allegiance back to the Republicans), would go no further than promising a voting rights bill.

King knew action was essential and turned to Birmingham, Alabama, a city with a population of 350,000, 40 per cent of which was black. Of 80,000 registered voters 70,000 were white. State governor George Wallace had become infamous for his slogan 'Segregation now, segregation tomorrow, segregation forever'. Between 1957 and 1963 seventeen black churches and homes had been bombed, including that of the Revd Fred Shuttlesworth, leader of the Alabama Christian Movement for Human Rights (ACMHR) and a founder member of the SCLC. The ACMHR had been campaigning against segregation for seven years, with minimal success. In 1962 (before the Albany events) Shuttlesworth invited King to lead an expedition to Birmingham. King welcomed the opportunity to test his tactics in the South's most

segregated city. Birmingham's public safety commissioner, Eugene 'Bull' Connor, had recently
threatened to revoke the trading licences of
businessmen attempting the minor concession of
removing 'White' and 'Colored' signs from
department store drinking fountains.

Success in Birmingham was crucial to King, not
only to demonstrate the validity of non-violent
direct action but also to rebuild his personal
credibility following Albany. In *Why We Can't Wait*,
published shortly after the Birmingham events, King
attempts to portray a smoothly organized operation, moving step by step to triumph. In reality the
campaign came close to collapse in its first days.

King understood the risks, telling an SCLC
planning meeting in January 1963 that he believed
'some of the people sitting here today will not come
back alive from this campaign'.[1] SCLC executive
director Wyatt Walker was dispatched to the city in
February to recruit volunteers and formulate a
detailed plan. At King's insistence the campaign had
four clear objectives that could be negotiated upon
once the action had been able, as he later wrote, 'so
to dramatize the issue that it can no longer be
ignored'.[2] The aims were the desegregation of all

department stores, the end of discrimination in employment and training, an amnesty for demonstrators, and the establishment of a bi-racial committee to oversee wider integration.

King's role at this stage was arranging support from other leading black organizations – NAACP, CORE and SNCC – and ensuring that funds were available to pay bail. He accepted a request from Attorney General Kennedy to delay demonstrations until after the spring local elections. Kennedy, like many of the city's black leaders, hoped for the return of a less reactionary City Commission.

Birmingham's voters elected a new and, in local terms, liberal mayor. Although Connor refused to relinquish his post as public safety commissioner many black clergy and businessmen, together with white supporters of reform, urged King to hold back from confrontation. King, clear in his own mind that only direct action could lead to meaningful negotiations, rejected their appeals.

Walker had recruited 250 volunteers, each of whom signed a card with the commitment 'I hereby pledge myself – my person and my body – to the non-violent movement', for the first day's march. But on 3 April to King's disappointment only sixty-five turned out. All were arrested, with Connor emulating the relatively light-handed policing conducted by Pritchett in Albany the previous year.

SCLC organizers hoped that the second wave would live up to King's threat to 'Fill the jails'. At an evening meeting on 5 April, King spoke to volunteers preparing to take to the streets. He urged them to forget their fear:

> Don't even be afraid to die. I submit to you tonight that no man is free if he fears death. But the minute you conquer the fear of death, at that moment you are free.[3]

The next morning forty-two marchers were arrested on their way to City Hall. By 9 April only 150 demonstrators had been arrested. The national, and even local, media showed no interest. King did not participate in the early marches, instead addressing nightly rallies, at one of which he was bitterly criticized by black businessmen. After only six days the campaign was faltering, with few volunteers coming forward to risk prison.

On 10 April the city authorities obtained a court injunction ordering SCLC organizers to suspend their activities. Unlike at Albany in the previous year, King had no doubts. 'If we obey this injunction,' he said, 'we are out of business.'[4] Courting arrest was essential to win publicity and keep the campaign alive. A thousand people lined the street as King and Abernathy led fifty-three marchers from Zion Hill Church towards the centre of Birmingham. King was arrested and placed in solitary confinement. When his fate had become clear King's wife telephoned President Kennedy, who returned her call after she had spoken to his brother. Almost at once King was given permission to speak to Coretta, who had only recently given birth to their fourth child, Bernice Albertina.

In his cell King produced one of his most remarkable pieces of writing, the 'Letter from Birmingham Jail', scribbled on scraps of paper. The document – a classic statement of his philosophy and a scathing indictment of racism – was King's response to criticisms by eight white liberal clergy of 'unwise and untimely' demonstrations. They called for him to use the courts and to negotiate. King replied that he too sought negotiation. This, he said, was the point of direct action, which 'seeks to create such a crisis and establish such a creative tension that a community which has constantly refused to negotiate is forced to confront the issue'.

King angrily swept aside their use of the word 'untimely':

> When you are humiliated day in and day out by nagging signs reading 'White' and 'Colored'. . . when you are harried by day and haunted by night by the fact that you are a Negro, living constantly at tiptoe stance never quite knowing what to expect next, and plagued with inner fears and outer resentments; when you are forever fighting a degenerating sense of 'nobodiness'; then you will understand why we find it difficult to wait.

There was, he said, never a right time:

> We know through painful experience that freedom is never voluntarily given by the oppressor; it must be demanded by the oppressed.[5]

Eloquent as King was, the letter remained for the moment private, smuggled out to SCLC organizers who feared that the campaign – still, despite his arrest, attracting little media attention – had failed.

What saved it was a 'children's crusade' and 'Bull' Connor's decision to drop the velvet glove.

The bulk of those arrested so far had been adults, largely middle class. With King out of touch in prison the Revd James Bevel and SCLC organizers began recruiting high school students and children. King, meanwhile, was convicted of criminal contempt on 26 April and released on bail pending his appeal.

On 2 May a thousand children and young people, aged from six to eighteen, marched out of Birmingham churches singing 'We Shall Overcome'. Over six hundred were arrested. The following day as further waves, chanting 'We want freedom', went into action, Connor's restraint collapsed. High-pressure fire hoses swept the marchers off their feet. Then Connor ordered in the dogs. Terrified spectators, many of them parents of the young people, pelted the police with stones and bottles, provoking them into greater violence. Scenes of women and children being hosed, clubbed and attacked by dogs filled newspapers and television screens throughout America and across the world. President Kennedy said the sight had 'sickened' him and later told King, 'Bull Connor has done as much for civil rights as Abraham Lincoln!'[6] Opposition to King in Birmingham's black community fell away. Connor had provided the crisis King was seeking.

As demonstrations and police attacks continued the federal government was forced to take a more active role. Robert Kennedy sent his chief civil rights assistant to Birmingham to encourage negotiations between the protest organizers and a committee of prominent white citizens, mainly businessmen. The Kennedy brothers also used private contacts to pressure business owners into making concessions.

With over two thousand protestors filling Birmingham's prison cells King declared at a press conference on 7 May that the civil rights movement had 'come of age'. The two sides declared a truce the next day but the white citizens' committee refused to negotiate directly with King, who was accused of being an outsider. Nonetheless an agreement reached on 10 May satisfied every demand that King and the SCLC had made. However, the last word had not been heard from white extremists. Following a thousand-strong Ku Klux Klan meeting bombs exploded close to the hotel where King had established his headquarters and at his brother's home on 11 May. Rioting broke out as police attacked angry young demonstrators gathering at the scenes of the explosions and then burst into black homes, beating and clubbing. Rioters destroyed nine blocks in the Birmingham ghetto.

This was the bitterness and frustration that King had worked since the Montgomery boycott to channel into peaceful protest. He and Abernathy toured bars and pool halls warning young blacks that violence was a trap, a game that authority would always win. Governor Wallace, meanwhile, dispatched state troopers to Birmingham. Fearing upheaval President Kennedy ordered three thousand soldiers to the outskirts of the city.

In the wake of the victory for King's philosophy of passive resistance this explosion of black anger gave a foretaste of a possible future. There was an alternative path to the one mapped out by King. The Nation of Islam activist Malcolm X, who rejected integration and had support in the Northern urban ghettos, argued that real change could only be achieved through violence and separatism. It was not enough, he said, to win the right to sit at a lunch counter.

In the ten weeks following Birmingham there were 758 demonstrations in 186 American cities, with almost 15,000 arrests. King himself, touched by the anger growing paradoxically from success, told a Chicago rally in June:

> We're through with tokenism and gradualism and see-how-far-you've-gotism. We're through with we've-done-more-for-your-people-than-anyone-elseism. We can't wait any longer. Now is the time.[7]

President Kennedy, criticized by King for his ineffectiveness on civil rights, accepted that only a promise of legislation could stem a summer of violence. On television on 11 June he committed himself to a new civil rights bill. Impressed, King was reported by the FBI as saying to Levison that Kennedy had been 'really great'. However, at a meeting with King at the end of the month Kennedy's tone was less friendly. The President said he had been told that Levison and other SCLC staff were 'agents of a foreign power', adding 'I assume you know you're under very close surveillance'.[8]

FBI director Hoover continued to report to Attorney General Kennedy throughout the summer on King's alleged domination by Communists. These were old accusations but Hoover added a new twist – transcripts suggesting King was a persistent adulterer – and described him as a 'tom cat'. Kennedy passed the material to his brother, with the note, 'I thought you would be interested in the attached memorandum'.[9] Hoover's reports placed the Kennedys, aware of the director's files on their own sexual affairs, in a difficult position, as was the intention. If the Kennedys allowed King to exercise too much influence over civil rights they risked accusations that they were carrying out Communist-directed policy at one remove. They would also be condoning what Hoover saw as King's hypocrisy: an adulterer who built a career on preaching a high morality.

Kennedy nevertheless continued his efforts with the civil rights bill, resisted, as he had expected, by Southern Democrats. He proposed federal powers to guarantee desegregation of public facilities and schools, to outlaw discrimination in employment and to establish government-financed training and education projects.

To build on Birmingham's momentum, and to demonstrate the depth of public support for legislation, King met the leaders of CORE, SNCC and NAACP to coordinate a 'March on Washington for Jobs and Freedom'. A. Philip Randolph had originated the idea and national organization was placed in the hands of Bayard Rustin. When President Kennedy was told about the proposed march by black leaders on 22 June he was initially horrified, fearing it would degenerate into a riot and wreck the civil rights bill in Congress. But as the possible political advantages became clear the administration worked to ensure the march's success, arranging food and drink and encouraging white unions and churches to participate. The organizers accepted changes proposed by the attorney general's office to a speech to be made by an SNCC representative.

A quarter of a million demonstrators – a third of them white – gathered in the capital on 28 August in a picnic atmosphere. King made the most celebrated speech of his career, watched by millions live on television. He had worked on his address the night before with Abernathy and Walker, but much of his impassioned delivery was improvised:

I have a dream that my four little children will one day live in a nation where they will be judged not by the color of their skin but by the content of their character. I have a dream, today! I have a dream that one day, down in Alabama, with its vicious racists, with its governor having his lips dripping with the words of interposition and nullification, that one day right there in Alabama, little black boys and black girls will be able to join hands with little white boys and white girls as sisters and brothers.

He concluded, emotionally, with many of the crowd in tears:

Let freedom ring. And when this happens, when we allow freedom to ring, when we let it ring from every village and hamlet, from every state and every city, we will be able to speed up that day when all of God's children – black men and white men, Jews and Gentiles, Catholics and Protestants – will be able to join hands and to sing in the words of the old Negro spiritual, "Free at last, free at last; thank God Almighty, we are free at last."[10]

Malcolm X dismissed the march, and the role the Kennedy administration had played in its organization, contemptuously:

They told those Negroes what time to hit town, how to come, where to stop, what signs to carry, what song to sing, what speech they could make, and then they told them to get out of town by sundown.[11]

Eighteen days after the march a white man threw fifteen sticks of dynamite into a Sunday school being held at Sixteenth Street Baptist Church, Birmingham. Four black girls died and twenty-one others were injured in the explosion. Fighting between blacks and whites spread through the streets as the black community feared this was the opening of a Ku Klux Klan pogrom. At a memorial service for the girls King condemned calls for violence and called on the congregation 'not to lose faith in our white brothers'.

On 10 October Attorney General Kennedy authorized the FBI to wire-tap telephones at King's Atlanta home and his New York office and the SCLC's headquarters. On 22 November President Kennedy was assassinated in Dallas.

SEVEN

'I DO NOT KNOW WHAT LIES AHEAD OF US'

King, like many others, was shocked at President Kennedy's sudden death at the hand of an assassin. He described it as part of a pattern in American life, a 'social disease' that included the murder of the Birmingham schoolchildren and the killing of black civil rights workers. But, politically, Kennedy's death gave King greater hope for the civil rights bill:

> . . . I think his memory and the fact that he stood up for this . . . bill will cause many people to see the necessity for working passionately.[1]

Despite the closeness that he felt he had developed with the Kennedys, King was not invited to the funeral and stood alone and unrecognized in Washington watching the cortège pass. But Kennedy's successor, Lyndon Johnson, acknow-ledging King's influential position, moved quickly to reassure him of a renewed commitment to civil rights. Within a fortnight of taking office Johnson promised King in the White House that he would push the civil rights bill through Congress with no compromise. King's status was confirmed when *Time* magazine named him the first black American 'Man of the Year' in January 1964. In a *Newsweek* poll 88 per cent of black Americans agreed that he was 'the most successful spokesman of their race'.

However, in early summer King met with another disappointing failure, partly due to President Johnson's reluctance to exercise federal authority. Civil rights workers faced consistent white violence as they campaigned to integrate St Augustine, Florida. Four people had died in Ku Klux Klan bombings and the Klan organized mobs to attack blacks attempting to share a swimming pool and beach.

King and Abernathy arrived in St Augustine in May and led a march to the former slave market in the town square. They were attacked by Klan members and the police. King, Abernathy and sixteen supporters were then arrested while attempting to get service at an exclusive white restaurant. King remained in prison for three days but accepted release on $900 bail to enable him to fly to New Haven to receive an honorary degree from Yale University. When he returned to St Augustine white defiance had brought the campaign to a dead end. Violence continued and the state governor banned night marches. King appealed for federal support. President Johnson refused, reluctant to intervene until the new civil rights bill became law. Disappointed, King departed, leaving St Augustine as segregated as on his arrival.

St Augustine confirmed King's view that the ballot provided the key to black influence, particularly in a presidential election year. He now concentrated his attention on Mississippi, where his Southern Christian Leadership Conference (SCLC) had formed a coalition with the Congress of Racial Equality (CORE), the Student Nonviolent Coordinating Committee (SNCC) and the National Association for the Advancement of Colored People (NAACP) to register black voters to support the newly formed Mississippi Freedom Democratic Party (MFDP).

Black civil rights workers had concluded that the sight on television of their white supporters being beaten by police influenced national opinion. In mid-1964 the coalition established a 'Freedom Summer' camp in Mississippi and encouraged white students from the North to train in non-violent action. To secure maximum impact, voter registration was concentrated in counties with majority black populations and with active White Citizens' Councils.

The Mississippi state governor denounced the campaign as an 'invasion' and promised resistance. Over the course of the summer forty black churches were burned, almost a hundred civil rights workers were seriously injured by police and over a thousand arrested. Violence reached a climax – and horrified white America – when three civil rights workers were murdered in June. They were arrested, released, then disappeared until their bodies were discovered six weeks later. Two were white and one black.

King called a 'People to People' march through Mississippi in protest against the campaign of constant intimidation. On their first night stop the marchers were attacked by police with tear gas and rifle butts. Re-forming the next day, the column marched into the state capital, Jackson, where it was halted and turned back by a cordon of police.

As the registration drive continued (by the end of the summer 50,000 black voters had been put on the rolls) King left for Washington to witness President Johnson's signing of the Civil Rights Act on 2 July. The Act forbade discrimination in public places (with a wide definition of what constituted 'public'), strengthened provision for integrated education and banned different voting requirements for blacks and whites. It went a step further than the original Kennedy bill by establishing a Fair Employment Practices Commission to combat discrimination in hiring workers.

However, rioting in Harlem, Brooklyn and New Jersey a few days after Johnson had signed the Civil Rights Act showed the growing pressure on King's philosophy of non-violence, particularly in the Northern ghettos. A further sign came at the Democratic Party convention later in the summer, when King's counsel of compromise met with opposition. The staunchly segregated Democratic Party in Mississippi fielded an all-white delegation at the convention. The recently formed MFDP, divided between supporters of the radical SNCC and the more moderate NAACP, sent a delegation of sixty-four black and two white members to contest the place.

The party's national leadership offered a compromise – the MFDP delegates could attend but not vote and in future segregated delegations would be banned. King, along with Wilkins of the NAACP and Bayard Rustin, accepted the compromise but two-thirds of the MFDP delegates rejected it and insisted on remaining in the hall, where they were ignored for the remainder of the convention.

Militants demanded to know why King had accepted the compromise rather than holding out. He had a longer-term view. King's objective was to strengthen the Democratic Party's progressive wing by forging an alliance of organized labour (he spoke regularly at union conventions), blacks and white liberals. As white Southern Democrats inevitably shifted to the Republicans the progressives would capture the party.

The criticisms levelled against King demonstrated that, for some, his programme was not radical enough. But King's leadership was winning admiration outside America. In October 1964 the

Nobel Peace Prize committee announced that he
would be awarded the prize for his success in
'keeping his followers to the principle of non-
violence'. At home the FBI was attempting to
ensure that honours were kept to a minimum. In
April the FBI dissuaded a Wisconsin university from
presenting King with an honorary degree by
providing information 'on a strictly confidential
basis' and another in Massachusetts by telling the
administration of his 'close association with a
number of secret members of the Communist
Party'.[2]

Hoover's agency, reluctant as King knew only
too well to investigate attacks on black civil rights
workers, had already worked to undermine his
position with the government. It went a step
further in 1964 by anonymously sending a tape
containing evidence of King's affairs with white
women to his wife. The intention was to provoke
her into suing for divorce. In November events
took a nastier turn. The FBI sent a copy of the tape
to King shortly before he left for Oslo for the
Nobel Peace Prize award ceremony. The package
contained an anonymous letter clearly intended to
drive him to suicide: 'You are done. There is but

one way out for you. You better take it before your filthy, abnormal fraudulent self is bared to the nation.'[3]

Given this background King was oddly, but perhaps understandably, conciliatory when he, Abernathy and other SCLC leaders met Hoover at FBI headquarters on 1 December. King denied that he had criticized the FBI, or Hoover himself, said he understood the danger of Communism and had removed Communists from the SCLC when he became aware of them. Hoover in turn claimed that the FBI had put the 'fear of God' into the Ku Klux Klan, so much so that in some parts of Mississippi he had heard his agency was known as the 'Federal Bureau of Integration'.[4]

A week later King was on his way to the Nobel awards ceremony in Oslo, stopping off in London where he announced while preaching at St Paul's Cathedral that he would donate the $50,000 prize money to the civil rights movement. At the ceremony he declared that the award, which he accepted as one for the entire movement, con-stituted 'a profound recognition that non-violence is the answer to the crucial political and social question of our time – the need for man to overcome oppression without resorting to violence'. Pacifism did not seek victory but 'to liberate American society and to share in the self-liberation of all people'.[5]

Johnson's landslide victory over a conservative Republican in the November 1964 presidential elections ensured the continuation of an administration sympathetic to civil rights. But the president rejected King's urging for a voting rights bill to underpin the registration drive. Johnson felt the South needed time to absorb the extensive Civil Rights Act. King disagreed and turned his attention to Selma, Alabama, to underline the argument.

Selma was a South Africa in miniature. Blacks constituted the majority of the town's 29,000 population but only 350 were registered voters. Public meetings were illegal and outside gatherings of more than three were banned. The SNCC had conducted a fruitless voter registration drive for two years, constantly obstructed by the local sheriff, Jim Clark. James Bevel, who had organized the successful 1963 Birmingham 'children's crusade', proposed that King should lead a confrontation with the sheriff to force the federal government to take action. King arrived in Selma on 19 January 1965, registered in the Albert Hotel (the first black to do so) and went on to eat in an all-white restaurant. At a march the following day sixty-seven people were arrested. The campaign had taken off.

King mounted a second march on 2 February at which he, Abernathy and 265 other demonstrators were arrested. The next day there were 550 arrests, including many of school children. From prison King wrote a 'letter to the nation' demanding federal action. With King in jail the increasingly radical SNCC invited Malcom X, whose philosophy was diametrically opposed to King's, to Selma. He advocated meeting violence with violence. The tensions between these two views were to break into the open as events in Selma developed. Two weeks after his visit Malcolm X was assassinated.

King was released after five days and the tempo of action increased. On 10 February 165 marching children were driven from Selma by Clark and his deputies with electric cattle prods. As attempts to register black voters at the courthouse were thwarted there were supporting demonstrations in towns around Selma. In one of these, on 18 February, a young black was shot and died after a local hospital refused him treatment.

King reacted at once, announcing that he would lead a march from Selma to Montgomery, 54 miles, to protest against Sheriff Clark's regime. But at a meeting on 6 March SNCC activists rejected King's plan and criticized him for leading civil rights workers into danger and then deserting them. Among the critics was Stokely Carmichael, who would emerge as a leading opponent of King's position. However, the threat of the march had an impact on President Johnson. He told King that he would instruct the Justice Department to draft a voting rights bill but appealed for black protests to be kept peaceful. Violence would alienate Congressmen, whose support was essential for legislation to pass.

As rumours intensified that King would be killed on the march, and with the state governor, George Wallace, saying that he would not allow it to proceed, six hundred demonstrators set out on 7 March. King remained behind. When the column reached Edmund Pettus Bridge it found its route barred by hundreds of state troopers. The marchers were given three minutes to disperse. The troopers then fired tear gas and charged, hitting out with clubs and bullwhips, injuring over sixty demonstrators.

They then invaded Selma's black quarter, beating bystanders indiscriminately. Next day the events of 'Bloody Sunday' were on television screens throughout the world.

Following Malcolm X's line many SNCC members demanded retaliation. But King announced that there would be another march on 9 March and that he would lead it. A federal court issued a banning injunction and Johnson, after appealing for King to withdraw, sent an emissary to negotiate a compromise. King, without informing the marchers, agreed that he would not attempt to cross the bridge.

At a church meeting the night before the march King said, 'I do not know what lies ahead of us. . . . But I would rather die on the highways of Alabama than make a butchery of my conscience!'[6] Heightening the tension in this way, knowing that he had agreed a compromise, was a dangerous tactic. When King halted the marchers at the bridge and withdrew he was denounced not only by the radicals of the SNCC but also by members of CORE, the NAACP and even his own SLC.

Ralph Abernathy, his closest colleague in the civil rights movement, wrote later, 'Soon, very soon, the advocates of violence would be saying that Martin was too timid to lead the movement, and then that he was too cowardly.'[7] The broad consensus that had been the civil rights movement's strength was reaching breaking point.

That evening a white clergyman who had come to Selma from the North to support the march was beaten to death by whites. The wave of anger across the country strengthened Johnson's position in promoting the voting rights bill.

On 15 March Johnson praised the Selma demonstrators at a joint session of Congress:

> Their cause must be our cause too. It is not just Negroes, but really it is all of us who must overcome the crippling legacy of bigotry and injustice. And we shall overcome.[8]

The words could have been King's.

On the same day the injunction was lifted, although the march – which was resumed on 21 March, with King at the head – was limited to three hundred people. Protected by federal troops the marchers reached Montgomery in three days. As numbers swelled to 25,000 King, his wife by his side, led the column into the city that had been the scene of his first triumph in 1956. 'We are on the move now,' he told a rally. 'Like an idea whose time has come, not even the marching of mighty armies can halt us. We're moving to the land of freedom.'[9] That evening a white woman civil rights worker was murdered driving back to Selma with a black passenger.

On 6 August Johnson signed the Voting Rights Act, extending federal powers to guarantee black Americans the right to register as voters. By 1966 430,000 new black voters had registered in the eleven Southern states. In the next two years two hundred black candidates were elected to office.

However, five days after the signing of the Act riots broke out in the Los Angeles Watts ghetto. In six days of violence and looting 34 people were killed, 209 buildings destroyed and 4,000 people arrested. The riots followed demonstrations protesting at police brutality, unemployment, slums, poverty and the impact on young blacks of the escalating war in Vietnam.

It was to the Northern and Western ghettos that King now turned, shocked by this rejection of his commitment to non-violence. He flew to Los

Angeles on 17 August and, while condemning the rioters, conceded that their rage was rooted in poverty and despair. In the same month King participated for the first time in a demonstration against the Vietnam war, the cost of which he declared was undermining Johnson's pledge to build a 'Great Society' in which poverty and discrimination would be eradicated.

As the era of civil rights legislation concluded, King moved to a wider cause, but one which remained consistent with the 'social gospel' he had adopted over a decade earlier.

'I CAME UP NORTH TO LEARN HOW TO HATE'

When King had first visited the North as a young man he had felt a sense of liberation at what he imagined was a lack of discrimination against black people. At a demonstration in Chicago protesting against the Vietnam war in August 1965 he was hit by a stone thrown by an angry white mob. At the rally afterwards he told the crowd, 'I had to come up North to learn how to hate.'[1] In 1966, as inner-city black anger grew, King was drawn increasingly to the Northern cities. However, there remained unfinished business in the South. In Mississippi in June 1966 King learnt that, as far as younger radicals were concerned, his time was passing. Prejudice would not be ended by black people kneeling in the streets, passively accepting beatings from white mobs.

In June 1966 James Meredith, the first black student at the University of Mississippi, set out on a march with four friends into the state to publicize the voter registration drive. On the second day he was shot by whites from a car and seriously wounded. At his bedside King and other civil rights leaders called an immediate three-day 200 mile 'March against Fear' from the spot at which Meredith had been gunned down. Shortly after the march set out King overheard young SNCC activists saying they would retaliate if attacked and when he spoke to them they suggested it was time to retitle 'We Shall Overcome', the civil rights anthem, 'We Shall Overrun'. The fracturing of the movement – and with it a rejection of King's strategy of non-violence – was intensifying.

At a meeting that evening MFDP members on the march unveiled a manifesto which demanded the use of the word 'black' rather than 'Negro'. Stokely Carmichael, newly elected as SNCC chairman, suggested that the march should be all-black and objected to the presence of white liberals. King dissuaded him from pressing the demand.

As tension heightened between what were now becoming two wings of the movement, Carmichael used the expression 'Black Power' in public for the first time at a meeting in Grenada, Mississippi. Divisions now revolved around a slogan – 'Black Power' rather than the SCLC's 'Freedom Now'. Carmichael's two words were resonant with meaning: black Americans would be forced to choose sides while the separatism implicit in the slogan excluded the movement's white supporters. Another leading organization, CORE, adopted 'Black Power' as a slogan while the moderate NAACP rejected it. Still respecting King as the movement's leading figure, Carmichael agreed not to use the expression for the remainder of the march.

The 'March against Fear' was peaceful until the 2,000-strong column reached Philadelphia, Mississippi. Here it was attacked by a white mob as police stood by. In Canton police tear-gassed and clubbed the marchers when they refused to move from the site where they had camped for the night. On 26 June the march entered Jackson, led by King, his wife and their two eldest children, to be greeted by a crowd of fifteen thousand. The bitterness of the divisions became stark when CORE, SNCC and the MFDP refused to allow

NAACP organizer Charles Evers, whose brother Medgar had been murdered by whites in 1963, to address the rally.

In King's eyes the movement was being torn apart with calls to hit back against white racism. White liberals, on whom his long-term strategy had always depended, would be alienated by the way the movement was developing. He rejected Black Power as a 'cry of dis-appointment'. He condemned demands for violence and racial separatism, calling Black Power:

> a nihilistic philosophy born out of the conviction that the Negro can't win. It is, at bottom, the view that American society is so hopelessly corrupt and enmeshed in evil that there is no possibility of salvation from within.[2]

On this the militants would agree. He dismissed as absurd the possibility of a successful black revolution in America:

> the power structure has the local police, the state troopers, the national guard and finally the army to call on, all of which are predominantly white.[3]

He called instead for the unifying slogan 'Poor People's Power'.

However, black militants such as Carmichael and Bobby Seale, who formed the armed and con-frontational Black Panthers in California in October 1966, rejected what they saw as King's lack of realism in calling on blacks to love their oppressor. King was booed by Black Power activists when he addressed a CORE/SNCC rally in Mississippi. Upset as he was, King had no illusions about the roots of the divisions. 'For twelve years, I and others like me had held out radiant promises of progress', he wrote, '. . . They were now booing because they felt we were unable to deliver on our promises.'[4]

Despite his position King had little choice but to respond to growing black militancy in the North. In the process there was an increasing radicalism in his words and actions. King could not help but be touched by the political and economic impact of the Vietnam war on American society.

In February 1966 he moved his family into a slum tenement in the black Lawn section of Chicago. His Southern Christian Leadership Conference (SCLC) was working with local black community organizations in a Chicago Freedom

Movement to attack poverty and discrimination in housing and employment. King went to the centre of the campaign, hoping by his presence to draw media attention to conditions in the Northern ghettos. He also saw it as essential if his philosophy of non-violence was to regain its faltering influence, to contest the increasingly powerful position of black militants. Perhaps as important was the fact that the headquarters of the Nation of Islam was in Chicago. At the end of February he met the Black Muslim leader, Elijah Muhammad.

King attacked Chicago's Mayor Daley (a pivotal figure in the Democratic Party nationally) for his failure to take action against the city's worst slum landlords. King appeared reluctantly to be moving towards the Black Power militants and in the process risked losing not only the white liberals but also moderate blacks. On 10 July, with little rest after the Mississippi 'March against Fear', he intensified the Chicago campaign with a 'Freedom Sunday'. After addressing a 45,000-strong rally he led a march to City Hall where he nailed a letter to the door demanding the integration of public schools, increased spending on education, construction of low-rent housing and support for black banks. He urged blacks to go to jail if necessary to eliminate slums.

King's attempt to transplant his strategy of non-violence to the North showed him to be out of touch with the depth of bitterness in the urban ghettos. Two days after 'Freedom Sunday' rioting broke out on Chicago's West Side following clashes with the police. Two died and a hundred were injured as black youths stoned police cars and threw petrol bombs. The disturbances ended with the deployment of four thousand members of the National Guard on 15 July.

On 5 August King was stoned by a mob organized by the American Nazi Party as he led a demonstration in support of integration through a white area. 'I've been in many demonstrations all across the South,' he told a reporter, 'but I can say that I have never seen, even in Alabama and Mississippi, mobs as hostile and hate-filled as I've seen in Chicago.'[5] While conservative blacks accused King of heightening racial tension by his activity in Chicago, SNCC and CORE radicals denounced him for reaching a compromise agreement with the city authorities in mid-August.

The campaign then moved its attention to employment, with the organizing of Operation Breadbasket under the SCLC's Revd Jesse Jackson. By the end of the year Breadbasket had secured nine hundred jobs through boycotts of white-owned businesses which had hitherto refused to employ local people in black areas. Despite this, King was disappointed with the campaign's overall gains.

The problem, as King increasingly understood, was structural. Radicalized by his experience in Chicago, the pressures from Black Power supporters and the effect of America's involvement in Vietnam, King realized that the civil rights movement had reached the end of one phase. Legislation had gone as far as it could – and President Johnson was willing to go no further. The King who had spoken as a young man of his 'present anti-capitalist feelings' appeared to be moving towards a form of Christian socialism as he called for fundamental changes in America's economic structure.

However, the Vietnam war was an immediate issue. Funds that Johnson had allocated to his War on Poverty had been withdrawn to support the cost of the war. Young blacks, the majority of whom were unable to claim the deferment from the draft open to college students, were disproportionately represented in the armed forces and suffered twice the casualties of whites.

In May 1966 a statement from King opposing the war had been read at a rally in Washington DC and he accepted appointment as chairman of Clergy and Laymen Concerned about Vietnam. At the Riverside Church in New York on 4 April 1967 he declared, 'Somehow this madness must cease.' He said he was speaking:

> as a child of God and a brother to the suffering poor of Vietnam. . . . I speak for the poor of America who are paying the double price of smashed hopes at home and death and corruption in Vietnam.[6]

His criticisms of government policy were attacked by the NAACP, his father and President Johnson. The FBI, which had always alleged that King was under Communist influence, intensified its surveillance.

In mid-April 1967 King warned prophetically that the government's failure to redress black grievances could lead to rioting in ten cities. Two months later 23 people died and 725 were injured in a week of rioting in Newark, New Jersey, and a further 43 died and over 300 were injured in Detroit, Illinois. King and other civil rights leaders condemned the riots, saying that they changed nothing but damaged the civil rights cause.

King's position was becoming increasingly precarious. Attacked by conservative blacks for his stance on Vietnam, he was booed and heckled by Black Power and white New Left activists while addressing a conference on the 'New Politics' in Chicago in August, despite his denunciation of capitalism, his call for a minimum income and his advocacy of support for Third World revolution.

In 1963 King had aroused FBI suspicion by declaring the common interests of black and white workers. Now, in December 1967, the SCLC announced that it would mount a Poor People's March on the capital to demand work and economic opportunity for the poor of all races. The march was due to arrive in Washington on 22 April 1968. 'We will place the problems of the poor at the seat of government of the wealthiest nation in the history of mankind,' King said.[7]

On 28 March King – more firmly committed to issues beyond civil rights – travelled to Memphis, Tennessee, to lead a 6,000-strong march in support of black garbage workers striking over discrimination in pay. King was disturbed on his arrival to find a large group of Black Power supporters on the scene. As the march set off they began smashing shop windows. King abandoned the march at once and called for his supporters to disperse. But in the looting and arson which followed, a sixteen-year-old black youth was killed by police, 60 people were injured and 280 arrested. King left for a meeting in Atlanta to plan the Poor People's March but walked out following an argument over tactics with Jesse Jackson. He returned to Memphis to lead what he was determined would be a peaceful march. It was here that he was murdered on 4 April.

In the confusion that followed King's shooting, the alleged assassin, James Earl Ray, was able to escape. Identified by fingerprints on the murder weapon, Ray was arrested at Heathrow Airport, London, a month after the assassination. He refused to give a motive but admitted that he expected to escape because he knew of FBI director J. Edgar

Hoover's hatred for King. At his trial Ray pleaded guilty – leaving many questions unanswered – and was sentenced to ninety-nine years' imprisonment.

A year after his trial Ray withdrew the confession, a position he maintained until his death in 1998. There were suggestions of a conspiracy involving FBI director Hoover, US military intelligence and a New Orleans Mafia family. As the thirtieth anniversary of his father's death approached in 1998 King's son, Martin Luther King III, had no doubt that 'the economic movement was why he was assassinated'.[8] The establishment feared the impact of King's move to the left as America floundered in the crisis of an unpopular war.

In the immediate aftermath of King's shooting, President Johnson appealed to civil rights leaders to keep their followers from violence and proclaimed 7 April as a day of national mourning for King's death. But the country was swept with riots as the death of the apostle of peace triggered the worst racial violence ever experienced in the United States.

King's body lay in state at his father's Ebenezer Church, where King had begun as a preacher at the age of nineteen in 1948. He was buried beside his grandparents at the all-black South View Cemetery. On his gravestone were the words of the old slave song, the words with which he had concluded his most eloquent speech: 'Free at last, free at last; thank God Almighty, I'm free at last.'

It would be easy thirty years on to dismiss King as no more than a 1960s icon, a figure, like his contemporary John Kennedy, of little genuine substance. Both effective media performers, each is remembered for a sound bite, King's 'I have a dream' resting alongside Kennedy's 'Ich bin ein Berliner'. It would be simple to say that King was a hypocrite, demanding the highest moral standards from others while he plagiarized his PhD thesis, committed adultery and had the books that bore his name produced by ghost writers. But King was larger than any of these faults.

Historians recognize that the civil rights move-ment in the United States was more than one man, that, as with all popular movements, it involved numerous brave and nameless individuals fighting for a decent life in local struggles. But for a decade King was the voice of those struggles, to his own people and to a white America largely unwilling to consider the crime against humanity that racism represented. During the Montgomery boycott one of King's parishioners said to him, 'Reverend, you have the words that we're thinking but can't say.'

King's overriding contribution to the civil rights movement was as a speaker and as a figurehead able to hold together the often competing factions that it comprised. He initiated few actions – the Montgomery bus boycott, the sit-ins and the Freedom Rides were activities that he joined or supported and spoke for. Even the crucial events of the 1963 Birmingham campaign – for which he is often credited – were organized while he was in prison.

As the movement fragmented under the impact of a disastrous and unwinnable war in Vietnam, when not only black ghettos but white college campuses were in turmoil, his philosophy appeared to have lost its relevance (and, to the media, its newsworthiness). However, King's commitment to a philosophy of non-violence transcended the civil rights struggle. It was to him a way of life with universal meaning rather than merely a useful tactic. It remained as relevant in the Montgomery bus boycott as it did when he moved at the end of his life to a broader canvas, to a confrontation with the poverty at home and the war in Asia that American capitalism inflicted regardless of the race of its victims.

King understood it is in the nature of an ideal that it may never be achieved but that a society living without an ideal condemns itself to a self-created hell.

NOTES AND REFERENCES

CHAPTER ONE

1. James M. Washington (ed.), *A Testament of Hope: The Essential Writings and Speeches of Martin Luther King Jr.* (New York, HarperCollins, 1991), p. 286.

2. Jules Archer, *They Had a Dream: The Civil Rights Struggle from Frederick Douglass to Marcus Garvey to Martin Luther King Jr. and Malcolm X* (New York, Viking, 1993), p. 180.

3. 'Letter from Birmingham Jail', in James M. Washington, op. cit., p. 301.

4. For details of court decisions and legislation see E.L. Bute and H.J.P. Harmer, *The Black Handbook: The People, History and Politics of Africa and the African Diaspora* (London, Cassell, 1997), pp. 308–21.

CHAPTER TWO

1. Jules Archer, op. cit., p. 123.

2. Taylor Branch, *Parting the Waters: Martin Luther King and the Civil Rights Movement 1954–63* (London, Macmillan, 1988), p. 48.

3. Flip Schulke and Penelope O. McPhee, *King Remembered* (London, W.W. Norton & Co., 1986), p. 20.

4. *The Times*, 10 September 1990.

CHAPTER THREE

1. *Liberation*, 1, April 1956, quoted in James M. Washington, op. cit., p. 78.

2.   Taylor Branch, op. cit., p. 140.

3.   William T. Martin Riches, *The Civil Rights Movement: Struggle and Resistance* (London, Macmillan, 1997), p. 48.

4.   Taylor Branch, op. cit., p. 185.

CHAPTER FOUR

1.   *Time*, 18 February 1957.

2.   James M. Washington, op. cit., pp. 197–200.

3.   Taylor Branch, op. cit., p. 250.

4.   Jules Archer, op. cit., pp. 139–40.

5.   James M. Washington, op. cit., p. 214.

CHAPTER FIVE

1.   William T. Martin Riches, op. cit., p. 66.

2.   Jules Archer, op. cit., p. 147.

3.   Taylor Branch, op. cit., p. 467.

4.   Flip Schulke and Penelope O. McPhee, op. cit., pp. 107–10.

5.   Thomas C. Reeves, *A Question of Character: A Life of John F. Kennedy* (London, Arrow, 1992), p. 34.

6.   Kenneth O'Reilly, *Black Americans: The FBI Files* (Carroll and Graf, New York, 1994), p. 187.

7.   Flip Schulke and Penelope O. McPhee, op. cit., p. 111.

8.   Jules Archer, op. cit., p. 148.

9.   Taylor Branch, op. cit., p. 613.

10. Henry Hampton and Steve Fayer with Sarah Flynn, *Voices of Freedom – An Oral History of the Civil Rights Movement from the 1950s through the 1980s* (London, Vintage, 1995), p. 113.

CHAPTER SIX

1.   Taylor Branch, op. cit., p. 692.

2.   James M. Washington, op. cit., p. 291.

3.   Flip Schulke and Penelope O. McPhee, op. cit., p. 123.

4.   Taylor Branch, op. cit., p. 730.

5.   James M. Washington, op. cit., pp. 290–302.

6.   Jules Archer, op. cit., p. 155.

7.   *Time*, 7 June 1963.

8.   Taylor Branch, op. cit., pp. 837–8.
9.   Thomas C. Reeves, op. cit., pp. 360–1.
10. James M. Washington, op. cit., pp. 219–20.
11. Henry Hampton and Steve Fayer with Sarah Flynn, op. cit., p. 163.

CHAPTER SEVEN

1.   Taylor Branch, op. cit., p. 922.
2.   Kenneth O'Reilly, op. cit., pp. 193–6.
3.   William T. Martin Riches, op. cit., p. 92.
4.   Kenneth O'Reilly, op. cit., p. 223.
5.   Robert Cooney, Helen Michalowski, and Marty Jezer, *The Power of the People: Active Nonviolence in the United States* (Philadelphia, New Society Publishing, 1987), p. 167.
6.   Jules Archer, op. cit., p. 168.
7.   William T. Martin Riches, op. cit., p. 87.
8.   Rowland Evans and Robert Novak, *Lyndon B. Johnson: The Exercise of Power: A Political Biography* (London, Allen & Unwin, 1967), p. 496.
9.   Flip Schulke and Penelope O. McPhee, op. cit., p. 205.

CHAPTER EIGHT

1.   Jules Archer, op. cit., p. 172.
2.   James M. Washington, op. cit., p. 582.
3.   Ibid., p. 592.
4.   Jules Archer, op. cit., pp. 174–5.
5.   Flip Schulke and Penelope O. McPhee, op. cit., p. 234.
6.   Ibid., p. 237.
7.   Jules Archer, op. cit., p. 176.
8.   'Who Shot Martin Luther King?', *Guardian*, 4 April 1998.

BIBLIOGRAPHY

All titles published in London unless otherwise stated.

Abernathy, Ralph, *And the Walls Came Tumbling Down: an autobiography*, New York, Harper & Row, 1989.

Archer, Jules, *They Had a Dream: The Civil Rights Struggle from Frederick Douglass to Marcus Garvey to Martin Luther King Jr. and Malcolm X*, New York, Viking, 1993.

Branch, Taylor, *Parting the Waters: Martin Luther King and the Civil Rights Movement 1954–63*, Macmillan, 1988.

Cone, James H., *Martin and Malcolm and America: A Dream or a Nightmare*, Glasgow, HarperCollins, 1993.

Garrow, David, *Bearing the Cross: Martin Luther King Jr. and the Southern Christian Leadership Council*, Cape, 1988.

——, (ed.), *The Civil Rights Movement in the United States in the 1950s and 1960s*, New York, Carlson, 1989.

——, (ed.), *The Walking City: The Montgomery Bus Boycott, 1955–1956*, New York, Carlson, 1989.

Hampton, Henry and Fayer, Steve with Sarah Flynn, *Voices of Freedom – An Oral History of the Civil Rights Movement from the 1950s through the 1980s*, Vintage, 1995.

King, Martin Luther Jr, *Chaos or Community?*, Hodder & Stoughton, 1967.

——, *Strength to Love*, New York, Harper & Row, 1963.

——, *Stride Toward Freedom: The Montgomery Story*, New York, Harper & Row, 1958.

Bibliography

————, *Why We Can't Wait*, New York, Harper & Row, 1964.

Morris, Aldon D., *The Origins of the Civil Rights Movement: Black Communities Organizing for Change*, New York & London, Free Press, 1984.

O'Reilly, Kenneth *Black Americans: The FBI Files*, New York, Carroll and Graf, 1994.

Ralph, James R., *Northern Protest: Martin Luther King Jr., Chicago, and the Civil Rights Movement*, Harvard University Press, 1993.

Martin Riches, William T., *The Civil Rights Movement: Struggle and Resistance*, Macmillan, 1997.

Schulke, Flip and McPhee, Penelope O., *King Remembered*, W.W. Norton & Co., 1986.

Washington, James M., (ed.), *A Testament of Hope: The Essential Writings and Speeches of Martin Luther King Jr.*, New York, HarperCollins, 1991.

Juan Williams, *Eyes on the Prize: America's Civil Rights Years, 1954–65*, New York, Penguin, 1988.

POCKET BIOGRAPHIES

Beethoven
Anne Pimlott Baker

Scott of the Antarctic
Michael De-la-Noy

Alexander the Great
E.E. Rice

Sigmund Freud
Stephen Wilson

Marilyn Monroe
Sheridan Morley and
Ruth Leon

Rasputin
Harold Shukman

Jane Austen
Helen Lefroy

Mao Zedong
Delia Davin

Marie and Pierre Curie
John Senior

Ellen Terry
Moira Shearer

POCKET BIOGRAPHIES

POCKET BIOGRAPHIES

Lawrence of Arabia
Jeremy Wilson

Christopher Columbus
Peter Rivière